SHELLEY &
CALDERON

SHELLEY & CALDERON

AND OTHER ESSAYS ON ENGLISH AND SPANISH POETRY BY SALVADOR DE MADARIAGA

KENNIKAT PRESS, INC./PORT WASHINGTON, N.Y.

SHELLEY & CALDERON AND OTHER ESSAYS

Originally published in 1920
Reissued in 1965 by Kennikat Press

Library of Congress Catalog Card No: 65-27128

Indexed in the ESSAY AND GENERAL LITERATURE INDEX

CONTENTS

**TO MY
WIFE**

PREFACE

THE four essays which form this volume are offered as a small contribution to the movement noticeable at present in this country in favour of a better knowledge of Spain and the Spanish-speaking peoples, the outward manifestation of which is the growing popularity of the Spanish language. There is little doubt that the driving force of such a movement is not of a cultural, but of a utilitarian, order. For the second time in history, the riches of South America fascinate the European, only this time the Conquistador stays at home and it is the enterprising Briton who stirs and dreams of Eldorado. The words of the Spanish language are thus the caravels which will take British trade across the seas and bring back—like the galleons of old—a less bulky though no less substantial cargo in the form of dividends. We need not complain. Commerce was ever the forerunner of culture, and the country which owes her first glimmers of civilisation to the Phœnicians and the Greeks is not likely to quarrel with the Britons. The merchant may build his ship for commerce, yet he cannot resist her charm, and falls in love with her. So the Briton may still fall in love with the Castilian language, though he learn it for purposes of trade.

From such hopes this book derives its inspiration. That poetry should have been chosen as the ground for this work of international goodwill may be due primarily to the author's own proclivities, but also to the influence of an essay on POETRY AND NATIONAL CHARACTER, by Prof. W. Macneile Dixon.[1]   Poetry is a subject which lends itself perhaps better than any other to such a purpose.   It is, like science and religion, a manifestation of the spirit common to all races, and it has over science the advantage that it demands the presence of our whole being, mind, soul and even body; and over religion that it includes within its sphere *this* as well as the next world. Poetry, moreover, is one of the human activities best tuned to the Spanish and to the English character, a fact which explains that both England and Spain should have excelled in it.   Lastly, poetry is an entirely unprofitable occupation.   It takes but little space.   It requires but little time.   It needs but little capital, and produces no dividends.   It can be quietly discussed without attracting an undue amount of attention.

The essays which follow connect English with Spanish poetry and character in four different ways.   In the first essay, SHELLEY AND CALDERÓN, the direct influence of one of Spain's greatest dramatists over one of England's greatest lyric poets is discussed, and an effort is made towards investigating the true nature of this literary

[1] Poetry and National Character.   The Leslie Stephen Lecture delivered at Cambridge on 13 May, 1915, by W. Macneile Dixon, Cambridge, at the University Press, 1915.

bond between the two nations by an analysis of the genius of each of the two poets concerned as revealed in their works and life. In the second, ENGLISH SIDELIGHTS ON SPANISH LITERATURE, a series of parallel studies of English and Spanish poets is used as a convenient canvas for the setting of a certain number of facts and opinions likely to stimulate the study of Spanish poetry in England. For, though we all like novelty, absolute strangeness has little attraction for us, differences being but spices which render more appetising the substance of our common human nature. The third essay, SPANISH POPULAR POETRY, is a study of what is perhaps the most typically Spanish creation in the whole field of literature, and an attempt at estimating the value and interpreting the meaning of Spanish popular songs in terms of English culture. The fourth and last essay—and perhaps the unwisest enterprise in the book—aims at showing the Spanish mind at work on a subject so typically English as the poetry of Wordsworth. When giving his—perhaps unfavourable—verdict on this last endeavour, the English reader should, however, take into account that in this case the " Spanish mind " happens to be working through one of its humblest impersonations.

It will be easily understood that, in the course of his work, the author could not abstain from expressing opinions on subjects such as English poetry, rhythm, language and character, about which he cannot claim to speak with confidence, still less with authority. For the sake of clearness, the style has been kept free from any wrappings of literary modesty, diffidence, humility and such other moral ornaments with which writers hope to conciliate the good graces of the critic, but which retard and irritate the reader. The reader cares not for the author but for the subject, and he likes to reach the almond of truth within the style without having to undo several layers of tinfoil. But if what the author has to say is said simply and directly, he, nevertheless, is fortunate in the possession of as much modesty as modesty itself will allow him to boast of, and there is not one line in this volume which is not written with the sense of the disproportion between his powers and the difficulties of his task. Nor is the writer impressed by the argument that his errors of judgment may be injurious to the cause of truth, for, even if his insignificance were not a sufficient answer to the charge, it still remains that truth in matters of poetical criticism is not a scientific and logical, but an æsthetic and intuitive fact. Hence, while errors in scientific method always result in loss of time, errors in artistic criticism cannot but help—ultimately—to the gradual delineation of truth. For truth in criticism is like a black and white drawing, in which the black shadows are no less instrumental than the bright spots of light in bringing out shape and relief. Let the author then be allowed to contribute, if only with shadows of error, to the shaping of the face of truth.

S. DE M.

SHELLEY AND CALDERON

To F. M. S., my Sister in Shelley

I

SHELLEY seems to have become acquainted with Calderón during the summer of 1819, while he was engaged in the composition of "The Cenci." Shelley says in his preface to his tragedy, referring to Beatrice's description of the chasm appointed for her father's murder : "An idea in this speech was suggested by a most sublime passage in 'El Purgatorio de San Patricio'[1] of Calderón, the only plagiarism which I have intentionally committed in the whole piece."[2] Mary Shelley, in her own notes to "The Cenci," adds : "He was making a study of Calderón at the time, reading his best tragedies with an accomplished lady living near us. . . . He admired Calderón, both for his poetry and his dramatic genius ; . . ."[3] From that moment right up to the day of Shelley's death, almost exactly three years later, Calderón and his works occupied a prominent place in the thoughts and writings of the English poet. The "accomplished lady" of Mary Shelley's note was Mrs. Gisborne, whom Shelley met in Livorno in May, 1818. Though Shelley felt an early friendship for this lady, who was an old friend of Godwin, his studies in Spanish do not seem to have

[1] See Note I.

[2] 'The Poetical Works of Percy Bysshe Shelley : with his Tragedies and Lyrical Dramas, to which are added his Essays and Fragments, etc.' Edited by his wife, Mary Wollstonecraft Shelley. Ward, Lock & Co., 1889. (Hereafter referred to as M. W. S.). P. 130.

[3] M. W. S., p. 159.

begun then.[1] It is not until after the summer of 1819 that references to Calderón and the Spanish drama become frequent in his correspondence and prose writings. He describes his Spanish studies in a letter to Peacock, dated Livorno, August 22nd, 1819 : " . . . . and at half past five, pay a visit to Mrs. Gisborne who reads Spanish with me until seven." Towards the end of this letter Shelley returns to the subject : " I have been reading Calderón in Spanish. A kind of Shakespeare is this Calderón, and I have some thoughts, if I find that I cannot do anything better, of translating some of his plays." While he was engaged in the study of his new discovery with Mrs. Gisborne, yet another admirer of Spain came to strengthen his enthusiasm. " Charles Clairmont," he writes to Peacock, September, 1819, " is now with us on his way to Vienna, and I make him read Spanish all day long. It is a most powerful and expressive language, and I have already learnt sufficient to read with great ease their poet Calderón. I have read about twelve of his plays." With his usual spiritual acquisitiveness, Shelley seems to have made Calderón part of his own life. He coins the word Calderonise,[2] and describes his steamboat in true Calderonian style, " our monstruo de fuego y agua." [3]

[1] A month later, writing from Lucca to the Gisbornes, he says : " We read a good deal here and we read little in Livorno," and there is nothing to suggest Spanish studies in his correspondence until a year later. That Shelley should read Calderón and plagiarise him after two months' study of the language need not surprise anyone. Spanish is an easy enough language for an English scholar, but, besides, " Shelley," says Hogg, " had always at his command a short and royal road to knowledge." (Quoted by Dowden, 'Life of Shelley,' p. 208.)

[2] Letter to the Gisbornes, Florence, November 6th, 1819. M. W. S., p. 135.

[3] Letter to Henry Reveley, Florence, October, 1819. M. W. S., p. 135.

Writing to the Gisbornes in November, 1819, he strikes an admirable image which gives the best and most accurate impression of Calderón's unequal art :

" I have been lately voyaging in a sea without my pilot, and, although my sail has often been torn, my boat become leaky, and the log lost, I have yet sailed in a kind of way from island to island ; some of craggy and mountainous magnificence, some clothed with moss and flowers,[1] and radiant with fountains, some barren deserts. *I have been reading Calderón without you.*"

The whole letter is devoted to the subject, and it ends with a quotation from " La Cisma de Ingalaterra," of which he says, " Is there anything in Petrarch finer than the second stanza ? "[2] In the same month he writes to Leigh Hunt :

" With respect to translation, even I will not be seduced by it ; although the Greek plays, and some of the ideal dramas of Calderón (with which I have lately, and with inexpressible wonder and delight, become acquainted), are perpetually tempting me to throw over their perfect and glowing forms the grey veil of my own words."[3]

Shelley's enthusiasm could die out as suddenly as it flared up. His admiration for Calderón, however, did not cool down with time and familiarity. One year after his first outburst of " wonder and delight " he sends to John Gisborne another of his beautifully expressive appreciations of Calderón's art : " I am bathing myself in the light and odour of the flowery and starry

---

[1] See footnote, p. 16.
[2] See the text of this letter in Note II, p. 36.
M. W. S., p. 139.

Autos. I have read them all more than once." In a post-scriptum he adds : " I have a new Calderón coming from Paris." And in November, 1820, he writes to Peacock : " I have been reading nothing but Greek and Spanish. Plato and Calderón have been my gods." When, early in 1821, Trelawny saw him for the first time at the Williamses, Shelley entered the room holding in his hand a copy of " El Mágico Prodigioso." The passage in Trelawny's " Recollections " is well known :

" Mrs. Williams . . . asked Shelley what book he had in his hand. His face brightened, and he answered briskly : ' Calderón's " Mágico Prodigioso." I am translating some passages in it.' ' Oh, read it to us.' Shoved off from the shore of commonplace incidents . . . he instantly became oblivious of anything but the book in his hand. The masterly manner in which he analysed the genius of the author, his lucid interpretations of the story, and the ease with which he translated into our language the most subtle and imaginative passages of the Spanish poet, were marvellous, as was his command of the two languages."

In September of the same year he writes to Horace Smith, complaining that the Gisbornes, despite their promises, had not sent him some books which he had asked them to purchase for him in Paris. He asks Horace Smith to do him the favour to buy them. At the head of the list, which includes " Kant " in French and " Faust " in German, comes " *a complete edition of the works of Calderón*," underlined by Shelley's own hand. Calderón is one of the names mentioned every time he writes down the great poets and minds of the world in his " Defence of Poetry." He has an interesting passage on Calderón and Goethe in a letter to Mr. Gisborne in

April, 1822, and on June 29th, a week before his death, he writes in a letter from Lerici : " I still inhabit this divine bay, reading Spanish dramas, and sailing and listening to the most enchanting music."[1]

Shelley's admiration for the great Spanish classic was, then, no passing whim, nor is it possible to explain it by an insufficient knowledge of the Spanish language on his part—undoubtedly a frequent cause of international literary admiration—for, as we have seen, Shelley admired Calderón with discernment, and could detect in his work " barren deserts " among " islands clothed with moss and flowers," and others of " craggy and mountainous magnificence." A genius is like an instrument of spiritual music, and when he awakens admiration in another genius it is as if the notes which he strikes stirred to vibration sympathetic strings in the spirit of his admirer. We may therefore expect to find in Shelley's lyre some strings in tune with that of Calderón. Their existence, besides supplying the explanation for Shelley's " wonder and delight " in Calderón, would perhaps help to illustrate the genius of both the English and the Spanish poets.

II

Calderón was a dramatic poet. His literary work outside the theatre is negligible when compared with his three hundred and twenty plays. These plays may be roughly classed into four groups : comedies ; dramas of honour and intrigue ; philosophical and theological tragedies ; and autos, or religious mysteries. The two

[1] M. W. S., p. 163.

first groups did not in all probability interest Shelley. They are perhaps the weakest part of Calderón's production, and add little to his value as a universal genius.[1] His greatest contribution to the dramatic poetry of the world is in his philosophical tragedies. It is these which Shelley meant when he spoke of " Calderón's ideal [that is, philosophical or metaphysical] dramas," and of which he obviously thought when he wrote :

" Some of them certainly deserve to be ranked among the grandest and most perfect productions of the human mind. He excels all modern dramatists with the exception of Shakespeare, whom he resembles, however, in the depth of thought and subtlety of imagination of his writings, and in the one rare power of interweaving delicate and powerful comic traits with the most tragic situations, without diminishing their interest. I rank him far above Beaumont and Fletcher."[2]

This comparison with Shakespeare[3] which recurs frequently under Shelley's pen is at the same time illuminating and misleading. Calderón is very similar to Shakespeare in the philosophical mood with which he unfolds the panorama of events before his audience, keeping, as it were, a running commentary on the current of facts ; also in that his characters are created from such a depth of inspiration that they usually convey a symbolical message as well as a dramatic emotion ; and in his eagle-like lyrical flights far and beyond the precise limits of the dramatic stage. The power of " interweaving "

---

[1] "El Alcalde de Zalamea," however, one of his best plays, belongs rather to the second than to the third group.

[2] Letter to Peacock, September 21st, 1819.

[3] Cf. "Wie viel treffliche Deutsche sind nicht an ihm zugrunde gegangen, an ihm und Calderón." Goethe on Shakespeare ('Eckermann Gespräche mit Goethe.')

comedy and tragedy is, as Shelley remarked, another feature common to Shakespeare and Calderón, but, while in Shakespeare comedy is really " interwoven " into the drama with the ease and grace of nature itself, it is in Calderón controlled by an almost scientific hand and ascribed to a definite function of the art of composition, that of *contrast*. In Calderón comic follows tragic as shadow the body, a manifestation of that dualism of Spanish art, which found its most celebrated examples in Velázquez, the painter of princes and idiots, and in Cervantes' immortal novel of the Knight and the Knave. This difference between Shakespearean ease and Calderonian control is not limited to the use of comedy, but, on the contrary, stands as an outward sign of the fundamental opposition between the genius of Shakespeare and that of Calderón. Shakespeare was free, and moved in the world with all the ease of a superhuman spirit, seeing all, accepting all, understanding all, with sympathy, equanimity and impartiality. His mind was as neutral to men's ways and thoughts as water to colours. He was a pantheist, and his view of the world was essentially æsthetic. His philosophy was poetry. Calderón lived in and for his Catholic faith. His ideas were strictly orthodox and his mind dogmatic. Almost all his plays are what the French call nowadays " des pièces à thèse," and the thesis is clearly defined at the beginning, often restated during the incidents of the play, and carefully brought to the foreground at the end to triumph and receive the crown of Eternal Truth. His art is not a reflection of nature. His mind is shaped according to a preconceived pattern to which things and people must adjust themselves. And this difference in

spirit naturally extends to form. The style of Shakespeare is free and spontaneous; it is like the very body
of thought, born with it. The style of Calderón is not
so much the body as the dress of thought. It often
follows a deliberate design, somewhat rigid and sym-
metrical, in which images and metaphors are set in parallel
order like the arguments of a barrister or the formations
of an army in order of battle. Thus, the same idea will be
illustrated by three or four successive images, developed
in stanzas of equal pattern; then all these images will
be gathered together in one final stanza, which rounds
up the argument and brings in the conclusion. The
typical instance of this method of composition is the
well-known scene in " La Vida es Sueño," in which
Segismundo complains to Heaven for having been deprived of his liberty, and successively compares his lot
to that of the bird, free to fly in the sky, the fish that
swims at liberty in the waters, the brook which roams
at leisure through the meadows, and the wild beast en-
joying an unfettered life in the forest, then in a final
stanza concludes asking: " Why was I deprived of a
blessing which was not denied to the fish, the bird, the
animal and the brook ?[1] The decoration of Calderón's
style is not less carefully studied than its pattern. Here,
again, the style is like a dress for thought, heavy with
gorgeous ornaments lavished with a truly oriental splendour. Yet, though his rhetoric appeals but little to our
more sober imagination, there is character and strength
in this style and a vivid glow which, indescribable and
untranslatable as it is, has been admirably felt and rendered by Shelley in one short sentence : " I am bathing

[1] See Note III, p. 38.

myself in the light and odour of the flowery and starry Autos."

But the profoundest difference between Shakespeare and Calderón is in the scope of their art, or, if you prefer, in their attitude towards life. Shakespeare is essentially a pagan poet. He lives in this world, loves this world, and makes this world the very centre of his art. He explores in all its depth and width the vast and intricate realm of human nature, but his man is the man of flesh and bones who dwells on our earth, the complete being— body and soul inseparably united—which we all are ; his characters are kings, fools, adventurers, rogues, lovers, maids and wives pleasant or unpleasant, people who move in the world in the manner in which we expect them to move according to their respective natures. He is king, but of a kingdom within the horizon of our earthly life, and if he now and then borrows a character from that which lies beyond, it is as a mere prolongation of an earthly character, like the Ghost in "Hamlet" who comes back to this world in order to settle with his heirs the matter of his enforced departure from it. "The Tempest" itself is but a pagan interpretation of the nature of man. Ariel is the spirit of life—of this present life. His business is as earthly as his pleasure, and who sang the pleasures of earthly life more exquisitely than Ariel ? As for Caliban, the symbol of natural primitive forces, he is not a spirit at all, but earth itself, brute, blind, violent earth, a meek but not loyal slave of life. And the tone in Shakespeare is that of the refined, slightly melancholical resignation of the later pagan, whose keen pleasure in life is tempered yet made more poignant by the sense of the fleeing of time. There is in

Shakespeare's elegant detachment a shade of renuncia-
tion which suggests that his soul has sought peace in the
sacrifice of the desire for Eternity.

Calderón is a Christian poet—nay a Catholic poet.
He would give the orthodox answer to Argensola's question : " Is the world the centre of our souls ? " In his
most famous play he pronounces this life to be a dream
and death a real awakening, and thus, by a violent stroke
of his poetical will, the position of Shakespeare is re-
versed and the stage removed to—

> The undiscover'd country, from whose bourn
> No traveller returns.

For Calderón, of course, that country is not undiscovered,
since it stands revealed by the Word of God. He moves
in it with as great an ease as, and with greater authority
than, Shakespeare does in this our solid world. His
characters are predetermined by orthodoxy and predestined to witness to the truth of the Catholic doctrine.
Even those among them which are not supernatural
belong to this world as little as possible, and seem to own
their life in the same provisional manner in which the
faithful are asked to possess their worldly goods. But
he often mixes in his plays, with characters of Time,
characters of Eternity, which easily explains his frequent
anachronisms, both of fact and of psychology. From
Eternity he is wont to borrow the villain of many of his
plots, as indeed was to be expected, since no earthly
character can vie in downright villainy with the Spirit
of Evil himself. The devil in Calderón is a most efficient,
ingenious and active villain, and one feels that he would
easily win every time he is about, but for his abject fear

of such things as Holy Water or the mention of the Holy
Ghost. This use of spiritual characters, good and bad,
reaches its highest development in the Autos, which are
little more than allegorical representations of Catholic
truths. The characters in the Autos are mostly abstract
ideas and categories personified : Thought, Liberality,
Charity, Death, Time, Avarice. No greater praise can
be bestowed upon an artist than that he succeeded in
animating allegory with real life. Calderón deserves this
high tribute, for his Autos, in spite of their allegorical
character, are intensely dramatic. It is perhaps in the
Autos that his most luminous flashes of genius are to be
found, and the finest examples of that " depth of thought
and subtlety of imagination " which Shelley observed and
so aptly described. Though inferior to Shakespeare as
an artist and a psychologist, he is perhaps bolder as a
creator and—when not childish in his orthodoxy—a
philosopher of greater depth. True, he was more favourably placed, for, while Shakespeare dwelt in Time, Calderón dwelt in Eternity—a subject of far ampler scope
for a creative genius. But in order to venture out of
this world without losing himself in chaos, an artist must
have wings of faith. Calderón's faith was as robust as
his artistic ambition required. He believes, knows,
asserts. No unanswered doubt ever troubles his mind;
no unsatisfied desire ever tortures his heart.

III

How can there be any spiritual connection between
such a man and Shelley ? The dogmatic, catholic priest,
setting upon the stage his theological principles in a

system of inflexible logic which binds even his style and metaphors into a rigid architecture, and the young and romantic revolutionist, the accurser of kings and priests, the poet, so impatient of all material fetters, so sensitive to wayward rhythms that he chose to sing of birds and winds and clouds, the lightest and swiftest wing-bearers in nature ? The somewhat morose depth of seventeenth-century Spain, what had it in common with the brilliant and agitated shallowness of nineteenth-century Europe ? How could the definer of faith appeal to the apostle of liberty ?

Yet, when comparing Shelley's work with that of the Spanish master, one is struck by a certain similarity of atmosphere. There is in Shelley's poetry a certain internal stiffness, an almost mechanical rigidity, which is at first the more disconcerting as it lies hidden under an admirably fluid external rhythm. The poet knows all the secrets of his art. His ear and his sensibility have been educated by familiarity with the best English and Italian classics. In poetical gifts he is second to no one since Shakespeare and Milton, and he has, over the two masters, the advantage of two centuries of development towards variety and freedom. We cannot therefore expect to find in him the same hardness of style which we observe in Calderón. But when due allowance is made for these contingent differences, we are inclined to follow up this internal rigidity of his poetry as a possible guide to the attraction which Shelley felt for Calderón's poetry and genius.

We notice then that this impression of stiffness, very vague in Shelley's lyrics, a little more definite in such philosophical poems as " Queen Mab " or " Prometheus

Unbound," becomes quite pronounced in the grotesque or satirical works, such as " Peter Bell the Third " and " Swellfoot the Tyrant." There are passages in " Swellfoot the Tyrant " which produce an impression as unpleasant as some of the systematic attempts at comic symmetry in Calderón. We are here at one of the points where Calderón and Shelley meet. Shelley does not understand comedy. He is not unlike Calderón in his incapacity for blending comedy with tragedy ; he is, in fact, worse, for Calderón could, if not blend them, at least mix them and contrast them in one play. But in Shelley, drama and comedy are strictly separated, and while there is not one ripple of mirth in that sombre tragedy " The Cenci," his sense of humour is so poor and his taste so uncertain that he sets out to write two poems systematically burlesque from beginning to end with all the patience and earnestness of a social reformer.

What his art reveals, his biography confirms. Shelley was as dogmatic in his revolutionary creed as Calderón in his religious dogma. It is possible to surmise—though not to assert—that longer years and experience might have softened the hardness of his convictions. But the Shelley who lived and wrote could undoubtedly give points to Calderón as to system and attachment to dogma. Loosely draped as she is, and softly as she moves with all the graces of modern art, his muse speaks in sure tones and with her doctoral finger up. We need not wonder, then, if Shelley felt attracted towards Calderón, whose own muse could speak with an unfaltering voice, as one who heard strains of a higher mood. The attraction was probably the greater for the fact that Calderón was sure while Shelley was only cocksure.

In this connection it is perhaps worth while noticing that Calderón's influence seems to have contributed towards rendering Shelley's style a little more architectural than his natural bent would have warranted. I venture to suggest that the composition of the " Ode to the West Wind " is the most brilliant example of Calderón's action over Shelley. Shelley wrote this poem when in the height of his fever of admiration for the Spanish genius whom he had recently discovered, late in the autumn of 1819. The plan of the four first stanzas is typically Calderonian : the first stanza might be called " The Leaf " ; the second " The Cloud " ; the third " The Wave " ; the fourth sums up :

> Oh, lift me as a wave, a leaf, a cloud !

Under the skilful and subtler development of Shelley the familiar style of Calderón's symmetric architecture is apparent, and the ease with which Shelley, perhaps unconsciously, appropriated a form of composition peculiar to Calderón is a very suggestive sidelight on the true nature of the spiritual relationship between the two poets.[1]

We saw Shelley " plagiarising " a passage in " El Purgatorio de San Patricio," and the fact that he should have chosen a Calderonian model for " a description of the chasm appointed for the murder of Cenci " is also very suggestive. Shelley's taste for weird scenery was

---

[1] There is another link between this poem and Calderón : the seventh line of the third stanza was obviously in Shelley's mind when he wrote to the Gisbornes the letter quoted on p. 5. The ode and the letter were probably written in the same month (November, 1819) :

"All overgrown with azure moss and flowers."—*Ode*,

"Clothed with moss and flowers."—*Letter*,

not unlike that of Calderón. Both seem instinctively to require for their characters and actions a setting of the wildest and most fantastic aspects of nature. Rocks, crags and precipices are their favourite element, and their muses, awkward and shy in the city, where Shakespeare and Lope have so many friends, recover their freedom of movement and their vigour of thought when left to roam in the boundless fields of fantasy. Both Shelley and Calderón are giants of imagination ; so was Shakespeare. But while in Shakespeare imagination seems to disperse, and gather in its light all the many-coloured qualities and shades of nature, in Shelley and Calderón it tends to soar away from the earth and to keep immaculate a dazzling whiteness of intellectual light. Perhaps this taste for the fantastic is, after all, but another manifestation of that mental stiffness, that almost mechanical rigidity which frames and somewhat binds the work of both Shelley and Calderón. For there are too many sharp corners in the city, too many winding curves in the country lanes, and it is only in heaven, where dreams can soar unfettered by reason, and in the skies, where clouds can fly unhindered by the highest steeple of man, that dogmatic minds find space for their unwieldy movements.

IV

Yet it is possible to exaggerate Shelley's tendency to recoil from the world of man, and still more to misunderstand it. Certainly no more frequent reproach is to be found under the pen of Shelley's critics than his so-called lack of human interest. Mary Shelley, his wife and spiritual sister, who did not perhaps understand him so deeply as is generally assumed, was the first to raise an objection against what she called " his tastes wildly fanciful, full of brilliant imagery, and discarding human interest and passion to revel in the fantastic ideas that his imagination suggested."[1] Mary Shelley it was who encouraged him to apply his genius to dramatic subjects on the ground that they give greater scope for the study and expression of human character. The same criticism is involved in Horace Smith's letter to Shelley (September 4th, 1820) : " I got from Ollier last week a copy of the ' Prometheus Unbound,' which is certainly a most original, grand, and occasionally sublime work, evincing, in my opinion, a higher order of talent than any of your previous productions ; and yet, contrary to your own estimation, I must say I prefer the *Cenci* because it contains a deep and sustained human interest, of which we feel a want in the other. Prometheus himself certainly touches us nearly ; but we see very little of him after his liberation ; and though I have no doubt it will be more admired than anything you have written, I question whether it will be so much read as the *Cenci*." Peacock, faithful Peacock, echoes the same opinion : " What was, in my opinion, deficient in his poetry was . . . the want of reality in the characters with which he peopled his splendid scenes. . . ."[2] This strain continues all through the century and reaches perhaps its most authoritative expression in the famous indictment of Matthew Arnold.

---

[1] These words were written as a comment on "The Witch of Atlas," which was the occasion for Shelley's poem "To Mary, on her objecting to the following poem on the score of its containing no human interest." M. W. S. "Note on the Poems of 1820," p. 278.

[2] Peacock, 'Memoirs of Shelley.' Edited by H. B. B, Brett-Smith, p. 71.

For Matthew Arnold, consciously or unconsciously, wrote as the spokesman of his country, the incarnation of the British mind. And as his moral and intellectual qualities and dominant tendencies undoubtedly entitled him to do so, his judgment on Shelley is an ideal document for the illustration of the contrast between the genius of Britain and that of her meteoric son. Being a typical Briton, Matthew Arnold is inclined to set up a moral standard above all other rules of thought or action. His attitude towards some of the more unpleasant episodes of Shelley's inexperienced youth is that of a British gentleman poking with the end of his stick into a rubbish-heap in search of some lost object. Yet, though this aspect of Shelley's life certainly left a bias in Matthew Arnold's usually impartial mind, it would be unfair to take a narrow view of his ideas on morality. His essay on Shelley is perhaps best understood with reference to his essay on Wordsworth. Speaking of Wordsworth's poetry, which he, of course, admired, he says: " . . . the noble and profound application of ideas to life is the most essential part of poetic greatness."[1] And he further explains his point by quoting Wordsworth's line—

On man, on nature and on human life,

as the subjects to which the ideas of the poet must be *applied*.

Thus, the essence of poetry for Matthew Arnold is not in ideas as such, but in ideas *applied* to life, or, as he himself explains, to the question of *how to live*. This is

[1] Matthew Arnold, 'Essays in Criticism.' Second series, Macmillan, 1888, p. 140.

the kernel of the matter, and a thoroughly British kernel too. It is—if I may use in a high and noble sense a word which is often most sadly debased—British utilitarianism in its purest light. For I believe to be a typical feature of British character (and I beg to be forgiven if I am mistaken) that the Briton takes for granted the things of before and after in order to concentrate on this world, and therefore devotes all his energies to life, its duties and pleasures and its organised progress. Who says life says action; who says society says concerted action— that is, policy. And Britons have discovered the best rule of thumb for concerted action, namely, that *honesty is the best policy*. Hence their predominant interest in morality.

Matthew Arnold was, then, a true interpreter of British character when he gave to his criticism of poetry a solid foundation of moral utilitarianism. Things must not be done without a purpose. Why sing for a song's sake? Why cry to relieve a heavy heart? Feelings must be husbanded by self-control and offered in a useful form to the community as a spiritual motive power for the social machine. Wordsworth, who did not err on the side of modesty, wrote on his own poems :

" They will co-operate with the benign tendencies in human nature and society, and will, in their degree, be efficacious in making men wiser, better and happier."

Note the word *efficacious*. This quotation ends Matthew Arnold's essay on Wordsworth, and its con- trast with the conclusion of his essay on Shelley could not be more illuminating :

" The Shelley of actual life," says Matthew Arnold, " is a

vision of beauty and radiance, indeed, but availing nothing, effecting nothing. And in poetry, no less than in life, he is ' a beautiful *and ineffectual* angel, beating in the void his luminous wings in vain.' "

It is Matthew Arnold who underlines the words " *and ineffectual.*" He was a trained moral engineer of this social machine which he did so much to improve, and his sentence on Shelley might be transposed in terms of social mechanics : " What ! Such a powerful pair of wings beating in the void for nothing, instead of helping to work the mill of morality ! What a shocking waste of moral horse power ! "

V

But was Shelley so lacking in human sympathy? Numerous are the incidents in his biography which prove his keen interest in the problems of collective life. He was an eminently political mind, and of the best British type, for he knew how to provide the ways and means for the achievement of his aims, and did not limit his political activities to pious wishes or brilliant theories. In Dublin he put at the service of the cause of the emancipation of Ireland his money and his own person with youthful generosity. He took a close and sustained interest in the affair of the Embankment at Tremadoc. He started a subscription in aid of the widows and orphans of the rioters executed at York in 1813, and while engaged in it yet another one to help the brothers Hunt, who had been fined £1000 for libel against the Prince Regent. He wrote a pamphlet, " A Proposal for putting Reform to the Vote throughout the Kingdom," and offered a contribution of £100 towards the expenses which his proposal would entail if adopted. He had definite ideas on suffrage and on taxation, and we have an amusing story from Hunt on his concern for the National Debt. As for his charity, all who knew him witness to the generosity of his heart, and, what is still more significant, to the efficiency and foresight which he displayed in his help.[1]

But it is not only in his life and politics that Shelley proved his truly British wealth of social spirit. The strong passion for justice which moved him to action inspired also his thoughts. His philosophy was little more than human interest sublimated into a system. All through Shelley's works his preoccupation of furthering the good of humanity according to his own lights is genuine and ardent. " Queen Mab " itself, which he repudiated in later years, though valueless in its philosophy is unimpeachable in its intention. And of the later poems, particularly "Prometheus Unbound" and "The Triumph of Life," there is not one of which it may be said that it is not inspired by a truly genuine human interest. But, as if his greater poems were not conclusive enough on this point, Shelley left a most lucid account of his views in his admirable essay on " The Defence of Poetry," a work in which the claims of poetry as a guiding light for the human race are understood in a spirit of such high and noble quality that it often anticipates by a whole century the present spiritual reaction against the economic materialism of the industrial age.

Yet, Shelley was pronounced to be ineffectual and lacking in human interest, and to this day that impression prevails. It is perhaps possible, without twisting the

[1] See Dowden, 'Life of Shelley,' p. 359.

argument into a paradox, to trace this misunderstanding of Shelley's poetry precisely to the passion for mankind which possessed his heart. His mind was not free to flutter here and there over the garden of human nature : he had far too stern an idea of his duties as a poet. " Poets," he says, " are the unacknowledged legislators of the world." His great poems are inspired by a definite conception of the world and of human destiny, and are written with the express intention of diffusing his sentiments and opinions among mankind. Though he says in his " Defence of Poetry," " Didactic poetry is my abhorrence "[1] he is a didactic poet as much as, or perhaps more than, Wordsworth ever was. His characters are not so much human beings as symbols, or personified ideas. He had a truth to serve, a theory to illustrate, a creed to preach ; and in this, again, he was the brother spirit of Calderón, whose Autos, which he so ardently admired, were also dramatised arguments, though arguments for a cause which Shelley hated with all his heart. The point was duly noted by Shelley himself :

" Calderón, in his religious Autos, has attempted to fulfil some of the high conditions of dramatic representation neglected by Shakespeare ; such as the establishing a relation between the drama and religion, and the accommodating them to music and dancing ; but he omits the observation of conditions still more important, and more is lost than gained by the substitution of the rigidly defined and ever-repeated idealisms of a distorted superstition for the living impersonations of the truth of human passion."[2]

[1] *Cf.* this remark on Milton's 'Paradise Lost' in the 'Defence of Poetry.' "And this bold neglect of a direct moral purpose is the most decisive proof of the supremacy of Milton's genius."
[2] 'Defence of Poetry.' M. W. S. Second Part, p. 6.

Far from being deficient in human interest, it is precisely because Shelley was too deeply obsessed with *man* that he could not write on *men*. His poetry did not dwell on human *character*, but only because it was overwhelmed by human *destiny*.[1] And that is perhaps why Shelley felt in Calderón a fellow mind, for both considered the human race as a whole rather than piecemeal, or in the multiplicity of its actions, and saw man, not on the moving screen of time, but against the immovable background of eternity. But within this analogy an all-important difference should be discerned. For Calderón destiny alone mattered, because he *knew* what that destiny was. Shelley, on the contrary, despite his external assurance, was in the dark, and his preoccupation was born of doubt and anxiety. He was too ardent in his humanitarian emotions to recline upon " the soft cushion " of doubt and smile and watch the world, yet he had in his English composition too high a proportion of healthy paganism to give up this world altogether and seek the key of the next for its own sake. Thus, unable to find serenity in resignation like Shakespeare, or peace in faith like Calderón, Shelley spent his short years hovering over the future city of his dreams when hope sustained the wings of his imagination, or, when hope failed him, wailing over his own misery and the world's wrong.

[1] The point is put with more acuteness than sympathy by Mary Shelley: ". . . even when employed in subjects whose interests depended on character and incident, he [Shelley] would start off in another direction and leave the delineations of human passion . . . for fantastic creations of his fancy, or the expression of those opinions and sentiments with regard to human nature and its destiny, a desire to diffuse which was the master passion of his soul." Notes to "The Cenci," M. W. S., p. 160. See Note IV.

VI

For this contrast between the assurance and assertive aggressiveness of the great philosophic poems and the dejection and despondency which weigh down most of his lyrics is, I believe, one of the most instructive facts in Shelley's poetry, the more so if it be remembered that the former were the conscious productions of a mind possessed of a determined theory while the latter were songs in which the poet poured his—

> full heart
> In profuse strains of unpremeditated art.

It suggests a cleavage between the conscious and the unconscious Shelley, between the philosopher and the poet. Shelley saw life as he thought it through Godwin's spectacles, but he felt it as it is in his own sensitive heart. The basis of Shelley's political philosophy is explained by Mary Shelley in her note to " Prometheus Unbound ":

" The prominent feature of Shelley's theory of the destiny of the human species was that evil is not inherent in the system of the creation, but an accident that might be expelled. . . . Shelley believed that mankind had only to will that there should be no evil and there would be none. . . . That man could be so perfectionized as to be able to expel evil from his own nature and from the greater part of the creation was the cardinal point of his system."

This theory rests implicitly on the assumption that the light of intellectual knowledge has but to shine on a man for his soul to be purified of evil. It overlooks the possibility that development in one direction may coincide with, or even result in, regression in another direction.

In its naive belief in the pre-eminence of intellect it makes knowledge the mother of virtue, defines vice as an error, and would fain imagine that sanctity can be taught in Government schools. It follows that even within our present imperfect age a man must be morally good in proportion to his intellectual lights, and that the higher his achievements as a man of science, a poet or a philosopher, the nearer he will be to that ideal type which we all like to imagine as the citizen of Utopia.

Shelley believed all this, and saw it denied by life in the case of three men whom he knew well—Godwin, Lord Byron and himself.[1] Here were three minds, a political philosopher and two poets, high above the level of common uninstructed men. Ought they not to be walking among mankind like luminaries of truth and happiness? Yet reality was hard. Godwin's sordid hypocrisy and the untimely death of Fanny Godwin, Lord Byron's degradation and the death of little Allegra in circumstances so dishonouring for her illustrious father, his own searchings of heart on Harriet's suicide—Shelley was too sensitive, too fond of the absolute, not to be impressed by these three shadows of sorrow cast by the three sons of light. For Harriet, though banished from his mind, was ever living in the innermost recesses of his soul. How could it be otherwise? We know that Harriet's suicide impressed him very deeply; "for a time"—says Leigh Hunt—that event "tore his being

---

[1] To this list might be added Southey, perhaps the earliest disappointment which Shelley suffered, and Wordsworth, of whom he said: "What a beastly and pitiful wretch, that Wordsworth—*That such a man should be such a poet.*" This last sentence (italics mine) is typical of Shelley's philosophy. The quotation is from a letter to Peacock, July 25th, 1818, 'Memoirs,' p. 131.

to pieces."[1] It was the symbol of the conflict between life and his doctrine. Shelley might explain away his crime to others and even to himself ; but the causes of it remained, and his secret wound reopened every time that life brought back similar circumstances. At every step of his wayward nature Shelley found his heart, which he wanted free, attached to life by threads of his own making. How often, seeing the cloud which his warm friendship for Claire Clairmont or his infatuation for Emilia Viviani gathered in Mary's eyes, how often would he feel Harriet's ghost rise in his heart and ask : " Are you the freer for my sacrifice ? " Thus little by little life undermined his faith,[2] and while he still sang his dreams of future bliss on earth in his greater poems, he gave vent to his despair in his short lyrics, free from the control of his dogmatic intellect. Curiously enough, there seems to be a direct link between Shelley's lyrical despondency and the intimate drama which he had to live through when his duty to Harriet and his love for Mary fought for the possession of his soul. Peacock[3] has recorded that at that time Shelley thought of putting an end to his life, and that he heard him say : " I am always repeating to myself your lines from Sophocles :

> Man's happiest lot is not to be,
> And when we tread life's thorny steep
> Most blest are they who earliest free
> Descend to Death's eternal sleep."

[1] Dowden, 'Life,' p. 353.
[2] *Cf.* "When I hear such things, my patience *and my philosophy* are put to a severe proof." (Shelley to his wife, Ravenna, August 7th, 1821, referring to the incident called the "Scandal of Naples" (italics mine).
[3] 'Memoirs,' p. 48.

It is illuminating to find the image set in the second line coming to light again in the "Ode to the West Wind," after a long subconscious stay in the poet's soul : [1]

> I fall upon the thorns of life ! I bleed !

It was this conflict between life and his doctrines which made him recoil from the world of action. In anticipation of the great Spanish play which he was to read the year after, he writes in 1818 :

> Lift not the painted veil which those who live
> Call life ;

and adds :

> I knew one who had lifted it. He sought,
> For his lost heart was tender, things to love,
> But found them not, alas ! nor was there aught
> The world contains, the which he could approve.
> Through the unheeding many he did move
> A splendour among shadows, a bright blot
> Upon this gloomy scene, a spirit that strove
> For truth, and like the Preacher found it not.

This tendency to convert his experience into a universal problem brought him to Calderón. He felt drawn to the Spanish priest by his deep religious spirit, for Shelley was deeply religious, in the same sense that a blasphemy is an act of faith. Shelley was in search of truth—not of those fugitive glimmers of truth which shine here and there in human nature and delight the detached eye of the pagan observer, but of the whole truth, a comprehensive and final scheme of the world. This and nothing

---

[1] See Note V.

less could satisfy his architectural mind. And while endeavouring to build within himself the fabric of the world, Shelley struck against the eternal obstacle—evil. His soul yearned for Eternity, but just as no one would love the sea were it not the mirror of the blue skies, so no one would yearn for Eternity did it not contain and reflect the Heaven of Perfection. And how could man be eternal when the best among men were made of metal so impure? There is a significant passage in Mary Shelley's notes to the poems of 1820.[1] " Shelley shrunk instinctively from portraying human passion, with its mixture of good and evil. . . ." That is, he had found out that puzzling fact of human nature that qualities and defects are like the roses and thorns of the same root-tendency ; he had felt, despite his theories, the depth and permanence of evil ; he had, in short, discovered the immortality of the Devil.[2]

VII

Shelley's interest in the Devil dates, it is true, from his early childhood. It inspired his favourite games with his sisters, and Prof. Dowden relates that one day he set a fagot-stack on fire, and gave as his reason that he wanted to have "a little hell of his own." This natural tendency, further illustrated by the fascination which from his

[1] M. W. S., p. 279.

[2] That this problem occupied him deeply is shown by the fact that he once thought of writing a lyrical drama on the Book of Job, as Mary Shelley has recorded in her notes to " Prometheus Unbound " (M. W. S., p. 125). The Book of Job is perhaps the grandest attempt at explaining away evil from a God-planned world. It is safe to surmise that Shelley would not have followed the orthodox version.

earliest days chemistry, magic and electricity had upon
him, may no doubt be explained at least in part by his
innate taste for the weird and phantasmagorial, yet it
prepared his sensibility for the understanding of the
symbols usually connected with the myth of evil, pride
and human rebellion against Fate.

Being himself possessed of a considerable dose of
satanic pride[1] he is most sympathetic to the fallen angel,
and in his masterful comments on " Paradise Lost " he
asserts that " it is a mistake to suppose that he (Milton's
Satan) could ever have been intended for the popular
personification of evil," and that " Milton has so far
violated the popular creed (if this shall be judged to be
a violation) as to have alleged no superiority of moral
virtue of his God over his Devil."[2] The same spirit of
revolt against the " tyrant of the world " pervades his
" Prometheus Unbound." In his preface to the poem
he explains why he altered the ending of the fable as
given in Æschylus : " . . . in truth," he says, " I
was averse from a catastrophe so feeble as that of recon-
ciling the champion with the oppressor of mankind."
The *champion* was Prometheus, whom he himself compares to Satan. The *oppressor* was Jupiter.

This was his way of avenging his own spiritual misery
on the sphinx-like spirit which caused it, for his natural
bent was Promethean. But that he was sensitive to the
more normal view of the myth of Satan is shown in his
enthusiastic admiration for " El Mágico Prodigioso."[3]

---

[1] An early offshoot of which was his refusal to fag when in school.

[2] 'Defence of Poetry,' M. W. S., p. 10.

[3] Not that the Devil in 'El Mágico Prodigioso' is free from that
Satanic spirit which Milton has immortalised. Far from it, Calderón

This drama is a Catholic precursor of " Faust," in which the maiden, Justina, is saved by her stout faith in the power of her own free will under the protection of the Christian God. The Devil, who had promised her to Cipriano in exchange for the young student's soul, unable to fulfil his engagement, sends him instead a spirit in the shape and attire of Justina, but when Cipriano lifts the veil which covers the coveted figure, he finds a skeleton, and hears a voice which says : " Such, Cipriano, are all the glories of this world."[1]

In a letter to John Gisborne,[2] Shelley compares the Spanish and the German masterpieces :

" Have you read Calderón's ' Mágico Prodigioso ' ? I find a striking similarity between ' Faust ' and this drama, and if I were to acknowledge Coleridge's distinction, should say Goethe was the *greatest* philosopher and Calderón the *greatest* poet.[3] Cyprian evidently furnished the *germ* of ' Faust,' as ' Faust ' may furnish the *germ* of other poems ; although it is as different from it in structure and plan as the acorn from the oak. I have—imagine my presumption—translated several scenes from both, as the basis of a paper for our journal.[4] I am well content with those from Calderón, which in fact gave me very little trouble. . . ."[5]

saw this powerfully poetic element in Satanic psychology, and rendered it in a fine passage (Jornada II, scene with Cipriano), which Shelley, of course, translated. And it is interesting to note how Shelley still emphasises the Devil's proud defiance in his translation. See Note VII.

[1] See Note VI.   [2] April 10th, 1822, Pisa.

[3] This may mean no more than that Shelley's own philosophy was nearer that of Goethe than that of Calderón. Yet it would have pleased Goethe, who said to Eckermann : " Calderón ist dasjenige Genie, was zugleich den grössten Verstand hatte."

[4] A journal which Lord Byron, Shelley and Leigh Hunt were at that time planning.   [5] See Note VII.

It deserves to be noticed that both in " Faust " and in
" El Mágico Prodigioso " Shelley selected for translation
the scenes where the Devil is on the stage. This fact
sets the seal to his poetic temperament. Francis Thomp-
son has observed that Shelley belongs to the metaphysical
school, and Mary Godwin records that he at first hesitated
whether he would devote himself to poetry or to metaphysics.[1] Poetry, metaphysics and theology are the three
avenues of the mind towards the problem of the world
in its entirety—that is, as Shelley and Calderón ap-
proached it. Calderón lived in times when theology
sustained the mind and heart of men engaged in this
superhuman task. Shelley had to be satisfied with metaphysics. While Calderón believed in his theology as in
the light of day, it was doubt which kindled that wistful
fire that shines in the eyes of Shelley's muse. Both
spoke in assertive tones, but while Calderón's tone is
unfaltering, like that of the Master who knows, Shelley's
voice betrays his anxiety to escape from doubt into self-
assertion, and quivers with the fear of darkness. And it
may be that, at bottom, what he most admired in the
Spanish poet was his possession of a key—though, as he
said, *distorted*—yet a key to the riddle of the universe.

VIII

It is a tantalising thought for a Spanish lover of Shelley
that he once contemplated settling in Spain. In the
very month in which he became acquainted with Calderón's work, June, 1819, he wrote to Peacock: " The
doctors tell me I must spend the winter in Africa or

[1] Notes to the " Revolt of Islam," M. W. S., p. 96,

Spain. I shall of course prefer the latter, if I choose
either." We may forgive him the last words of the
sentence, for indifference is the most we are accustomed
to expect from Englishmen who have never been in
Spain, and we know how easily English indifference,
under the sun of Spain, flames up into English enthusiasm.
Had Shelley carried out his plan I firmly believe his
genius would have attained the almost superhuman
height and depth of which he left us but a promise.
Mary Shelley says of him : " As a poet his intellect and
compositions were powerfully influenced by exterior
circumstances, and especially by his place of abode."
Spain, and particularly the central tableland of Castile,
is a most admirable environment for men of deep spiritual
life, and we have a striking example of her power to stamp
her seal on foreign minds in the art of El Greco. The
temptation to indulge in this perhaps idle dream of asso-
ciating Shelley and El Greco and the spirit of Spain is
too strong, especially after reading Shelley's remarks on
Michael Angelo's Day of Judgment. Listen :

" On one side of this figure are the elect ; on the other the
host of heaven ; they ought to have been what the Christians
call *glorified bodies*, floating onward and radiant with that everlasting light (I speak in the spirit of their faith) which had consumed their mortal veil. They are in fact very ordinary people."[1]

" *Floating onward and radiant with everlasting light !* "
There never was a happier description of El Greco's
religious pictures than these prophetic[2] words, so steeped

[1] Letter to Peacock, ' Memoirs,' p. 174.

[2] Prophetic, because El Greco was not born to universal Art until he
was re-discovered by Señor Cossío in relatively recent times. Pacheco
records that once El Greco, in conversation with him, said of Michael
Angelo that "he was a good fellow but he could not paint." (Quoted by
Cossío ' El Greco,' p. 345.)

in the spirit of the mystical painter whom they seem to have divined across time and space.[1] Higher than in sensuous Naples or even in the exquisite and intellectual Florence, Shelley's genius would have risen in Toledo, Avila, Salamanca, any of those Castilian towns which seem dead but are deep in their quietness, like wells. In Italy his romantic tendency towards the gratification of desire was stimulated by the loveliness and womanliness of Nature itself; but in the austere grandeur of the Castilian tableland, in its immense horizon, its vast solitude, its calm, which seems to stretch beyond the bounds of space and time, Shelley would have found an atmosphere more in harmony with his metaphysical soul. Though the more graceful and pagan side of his nature might have suffered, he would have gained in depth and strength, and his genius, less solicited by the lighter and more fanciful muses, might have conceived the " Paradise Lost " of the nineteenth century—the poem of the *Spirit who strove for Truth and found it not.*

[1] Shelley's famous epithets on Calderón, "the flowery and starry Autos" apply even more accurately to the Art of El Greco. No more exquisite description could be given of such pictures as 'El Entierro del Conde de Orgaz.'

As will be seen, Shelley followed his Spanish model very closely. It occurs in Jornada II, Scene 19, of " El Purgatorio de San Patricio." The last line of Calderón has been literally translated by Shelley.

> ¿ No ves ese peñasco, que parece
> Que se está sustentando con trabajo,
> Y con el ansia misma que padece,
> Há tantos siglos que se viene abajo ?
> Pues mordaza es que sella y enmudece
> El aliento a una boca que debajo
> Abierta está, por donde con pereza
> El monte melancólico bosteza.

Here is Shelley's rendering in " The Cenci," Act III, Scéne 1 :

> Two miles on this side of the fort, the road
> Crosses a deep ravine ; 'tis rough and narrow,
> And winds with short turns down the precipice ;
> And in its depth there is a mighty rock,
> Which has, from unimaginable years,
> Sustained itself with terror and with toil
> Over a gulf, and with the agony
> With which it clings seems slowly coming down ;
> Even as a wretched soul hour after hour
> Clings to the mass of life ; yet, clinging, leans ;
> And, leaning, makes more dark the dread abyss
> In which it fears to fall : beneath this crag
> Huge as despair, as if in weariness,
> The melancholy mountain yawns. . . ,

NOTE II

FLORENCE,

Nov. 16, 1819.

" MADONNA,

"I have been lately voyaging in a sea without my pilot, and although my sail has often been torn, my boat become leaky, and the log lost, I have yet sailed in a kind of way from island to island; some of craggy and mountainous magnificence, some clothed with moss and flowers, and radiant with fountains, some barren deserts. *I have been reading Calderón without you.* I have read the 'Cisma de Ingalaterra,' the 'Cabellos de Absolom' and three or four others. These pieces, inferior to those we read, at least to the 'Principe Constante,' in the splendour of particular passages, are perhaps superior in their satisfying completeness. The 'Cabellos de Absolom' is full of the deepest and tenderest touches of nature. Nothing can be more pathetically conceived than the character of old David, and the tender and impartial love, overcoming all insults and all crimes, with which he regards his conflicting and disobedient sons. The incest scene of Amnon and Tamar is perfectly tremendous. Well may Calderón say in the person of the former—

> Si sangre sin fuego hiere,[1]
> Que fara sangre con fuego ¿

Incest is, like many other incorrect things, a very poetical circumstance. It may be the excess of love or hate. It may be the defiance of everything for the sake of another, which clothes itself in the glory of the highest heroism; or it may be that cynical rage which, confounding the good and the bad in existing opinions, breaks through them for the purpose of rioting in selfishness and antipathy. Calderón, following the Jewish historians, has represented Amnon's action in the basest

---

[1] Mary Shelley gives *hiere* (wounds). The text is, of course, *hierve* (boils).

point of view—he is a prejudiced savage, acting what he abhors and abhorring that which is the unwilling party to his crime.

            " Adieu, Madonna,
                    " Yours truly,
                            " P. B. S."

I transcribe you a passage from the " Cisma de Ingalaterra," spoken by " Carlos, Embaxador de Francia, enamorado de Ana Bolena." Is there anything in Petrarch finer than the second stanza ? [1]

> Porque apenas el sol se coronaba
> De nueva luz en la estacion primera
> Quando yo en sus umbrales adoraba
> Segundo sol en abreviada esfera ;
> La noche apenas trémula baxaba,
> A solos mis deseos lisonjera,
> Quando un jardin, republica de flores,
> Era tercero fiel de mis amores.
>
> Alli, el silencio de la noche fria,
> El jazmin que en las redes se enlazava,
> El cristal de la fuente que corria,
> El arroyo que a solas murmurava,
> El viento que en las hojas se movia,
> El Aura que en las flores respirava ;
> Todo era amor ; què mucho, si en tal calma,
> Aves, fuentes y flores tienen alma !
>
> No has visto providente y officiosa,
> Mover el ayre iluminada aveja,
> Que hasta beber la purpura a la rosa
> Ya se acerca cobarde, y ya se alexa ?
> No has visto enamorada mariposa,

---

[1] The spelling of Shelley as given by Mary Shelley has been respected.

Dar cercos a la luz, hasta que dexa,
En monumento facil abrasadas
Las alas de color tornasoladas ?

Assi mi amor, cobarde muchos dias,
Tornos hizo a la rosa y a la llama ;
Temor che ha sido entre cenizas frias,
Tantas vezes llorado de quien ama ;
Pero el amor, que vence con porfias,
Y la ocasion, que con disculpas llama,
Me animaron, y aveja y mariposa
Quemè las alas, y lleguè a la rosa.

NOTE III

Here is the text of this famous scene, together with a translation by Archbishop Trench, which unfortunately misses out the last or " summing up " stanza.

¡ Ay mísero de mí ¡ ¡ ay infelice !	Ah ! miserable me, ah, woe, woe, woe !
Apurar, cielos, pretendo,	Heavens, why make ye me to mourn,
Ya que me tratais así,	More than all men else forlorn ?
Qué delito cometí	If my birth has been my sin,
Contra vosotros naciendo :	Yet what sinned I more herein
Aunque si nací, ya entiendo,	Than others, who were also born ?
Qué delito he cometido :	. . . . . .
Bastante causa ha tenido	
Vuestra justicia y rigor,	. . . . . .
Pues el delito mayor	
Del hombre es haber nacido.	. . . . . .
Sólo quisiera saber,	

Para apurar mis desvelos,
(Dejando a una parte, cielos,
El delito de nacer)
¿Qué más os pude ofender,
Para castigarme más?
¿No nacieron los demás?
Pues si los demás nacieron,
¿Qué privilegios tuvieron,
Que yo no gocé jamás?

Nace el ave, y con las galas

Que le dan belleza suma,
Apenas es flor de pluma,
O ramillete con alas,
Cuando las etéreas salas
Corta con velocidad,
Negándose a la piedad
Del nido que deja en calma;
Y teniendo yo mas alma,
Tengo menos libertad.

Nace el bruto y con la piel,

Que dibujan manchas bellas,

Apenas signo es de estrellas,
(Gracias al docto pincel)

Cuando atrevido y cruel
La humana necesidad
Le enseña a tener crueldad,
Monstruo de su laberinto;
Y yo con mejor instinto
Tengo menos libertad.

Nace el pez, que no respira,
Aborto de ovas y lamas,

Born the bird was, yet with gay
Gala vesture, beauty's dower,
Scarcely 'tis a wingéd flower,
Or a richly-plumaged spray,
Ere the aërial halls of day
It divideth rapidly,
And no more will debtor be
To the nest it hastes to quit;
But with more of soul than it,
I am grudged its liberty.

And the beast was born, whose skin
Scarce those beauteous spots and bars
Like to constelled stars
Doth from its great Painter win,
Ere the instinct doth begin
Of its fierceness and its pride,
And its lair on every side
It has measured far and nigh;
While with better instinct I
Am its liberty denied.

Born the mute fish was also,
Child of ooze and ocean weed;

Y apenas, bajel de escamas,
Sobre las ondas se mira,
Cuando a todas partes gira,
Midiendo la inmensidad
De tanta capacidad
Como le da el centro frío ;
Y yo con mas albedrío

Tengo menos libertad.
Nace el arroyo, culebra

Que entre flores se desata,

Y apenas, sierpe de plata,
Entre las flores se quiebra,

Cuando músico celebra
De las flores la piedad,
Que le da la majestad
El campo abierto a su huida ;
Y teniendo yo mas vida,
Tengo menos libertad.
En llegando a esta pasión,
Un volcán, un Etna hecho,
Quisiera arrancar del pecho
Pedazos del corazón :
¿ Qué ley, justicia o razón
Negar a los hombres sabe
Privilegio tan suave,
Excepción tan principal,
Que Dios le ha dado a un
    cristal,
A un pez, a un bruto y a un
    ave ?

Scarce a finny bark of speed
To the surface brought, and lo!
In vast circuits to and fro
Measures it on every side
All the waste of ocean wide,
Its illimitable home ;
While with greater will to
    roam
I that freedom am denied.
Born the streamlet was, a
    snake
Which unwinds the flowers
    among,
Silver serpent that not long
May to them sweet music
    make
Ere it quits the flow'ry brake
Onward hastening to the sea
With majestic course and free,
Which the open plains supply ;
While with more life gifted, I
Am denied its liberty.

.   .   .   .   .

.   .   .   .   .

.   .   .   .   .

.   .   .   .   .

Shelley translated from "El Mágico Prodigioso" a passage written in this kind of pattern. Called forth by the Devil, the spirits of Love are tempting Justina. Here is the Spanish text and Shelley's translation, which, as will be noticed, does not strictly conform to the symmetry of the original.

Voz cant.	The First Voice.
No hay sugeto en qué no imprima	There is no form in which the fire
El fuego de amor su llama ;	Of love its traces has impressed not ;
Pues vive más donde ama	Man lives far more in love's desire
El hombre, que donde anima.	Than by life's breath soon possessed not.
Amor solamente estima	If all that lives must love or die,
Cuanto tener vida sabe,	All shapes on earth, or sea, or sky
El tronco, la flor y el ave :	With one consent to Heaven cry
Luego es la gloria mayor	That the glory far above
Desta vida . . .	All else in life is—
TODOS : Amor, amor.	ALL : Love, O, Love !

JUSTINA.	JUSTINA.
Pesada imaginación,	Thou, melancholy thought which art
Al parecer lisonjera,	So fluttering and so sweet, to thee
¿ Cúando te he dado ocasión, Para que desta manera Aflijas mi corazón ?	When did I give the liberty Thus to afflict my heart ? What is the cause of this new power

¿Cuál es la causa, en rigor,

Deste fuego, deste ardor,

Que en mi por instantes
    crece?
¿Qué dolor el que padece

Mi sentido?
TODOS: Amor, amor.

JUSTINA.

Aquel ruiseñor amante

Es quien respuesta me da,
Enamorando constante
A su consorte, que está
Un ramo mas adelante.

Calla ruiseñor; no aquí

Imaginar me hagas ya,
Por las quejas que te oí,

Cómo un hombre sentirá,
Si siente un pájaro así.
Mas nó; una vid fué lasciva,
Que buscando fugitiva

Va el tronco donde se enlace,
Siendo el verdor con que
    abrace,
El peso con que derriba.

Which doth my fevered being
    move,
Momently raging more and
    more?
What subtle pain is kindled
    now
Which from my heart doth
    overflow
Into my senses?—
ALL: Love, O Love!

JUSTINA.

'Tis that enamoured nightin-
    gale
Who gives me the reply,
He ever tells the same soft tale
Of passion and of constancy
To his mate, who, rapt and
    fond,
Listening sits, a bough beyond.
Be silent, Nightingale! No
    more
Make me think, in hearing thee
Thus tenderly thy love de-
    plore,
If a bird can feel his so,
What a man would feel for me.
And, voluptuous vine, O thou
Who seekest most when least
    pursuing,
To the trunk thou interlacest,
Art the verdure which em-
    bracest,
And the weight which is its
    ruin,

No así con verdes abrazos	No more, with green embraces, vine,
Me hagas pensar en quién amas,	Make me think on what thou lovest,
Vid; que dudaré en tus lazos,	For whilst thou thus thy boughs entwine
Si asi abrazan unas ramas,	I fear lest thou should'st teach me, sophist,
Cómo enraman unos brazos.	How arms might be entangled too.
Y si no es la vid, será	Light-enchanted sunflower, thou
Aquel girasol, que está	Who gazest ever true and tender
Viendo cara a cara al sol,	On the sun's revolving splendour,
Tras cuyo hermoso arrebol	Follow not his faithless glance
Siempre moviéndose va.	With thy faded countenance,
No sigas, nó, tus enojos,	Nor teach my beating heart to fear,
Flor, con marchitos despojos;	If leaves can mourn without a tear,
Que pensaran mis congojas,	How eyes must weep. . . .
Si asi lloran unas hojas,	. . . . . .
Como lloran unos ojos.	. . . O, Nightingale,
Cesa, amante ruiseñor,	Cease from thy enamoured tale—
Desúnete, vid frondosa,	Leafy vine, unwreath thy bower,
Párate, insconstante flor,	Restless sunflower, cease to move,
O decid, ¿qué venenosa	Or tell me all, what poisonous power
Fuerza usáis?	Ye use against me—
TODOS: Amor, amor.	ALL: Love! love! love!

NOTE IV

This opposition between character and destiny is somewhat parallel to that between individualistic tendencies and social tendencies in man. Character is the side of human nature which most interests society; destiny, the individual. Thus the reproach addressed to Shelley by practically all his British critics might be considered as one more sign of the eminently social or moral type of mind prevalent in the Anglo-Saxon race in modern times. We have seen Mary Shelley showing her peculiarly British tendencies in this connection, and urging her husband to devote his powers to the delineation of human character—that is, to dramatic poetry. But nothing could be more typical of Shelley's strong individualism than his adventure as a playwright. Of " The Cenci " Peacock said :

> " He only once descended into the arena of reality, and that was in the tragedy of ' The Cenci.' This is unquestionably a work of great dramatic power, but it is unquestionably not a work for the modern English stage."

Why ? Because its subject is not of a moral or social type. It is certainly *character*, but of a nature which makes it extremely anti-social. " The Cenci " deals with a case of incest. It is a subject that fascinated Shelley. In his letter, already quoted in Note II, to Mrs. Gisborne, he comments on " Los Cabellos de Absolom "—another incest play—in the following words :

> " The incest scene of ' Amnon and Tamar ' is perfectly tremendous. . . . Incest is, like many other incorrect things, a very poetical circumstance. It may be the excess of love or hate. It may be the defiance of everything for the sake of another, which clothes itself in the glory of the highest heroism ; or it may be that cynical rage which, confounding the good and the bad in existing opinions, breaks through

them for the purpose of rioting in selfishness and anti-pathy."

That is the claim of the individualistic artist, who seeks to recreate in his art whatever lives in the soul of man. Society is not his concern, but man and his destiny. And for the problem of destiny, the soul of a great criminal is at least as good a path of approach as that of a shepherd. For the opposite view we may turn to Archbishop Trench:

> " Painful I have called the play (' El Alcalde de Zalamea '), in that, like Southey's ' Roderick the Goth,' it turns on a crime so revolting as utterly to disqualify it from constituting the turning point in a work of art—even as I must consider Shelley's ' Cenci,' which adds a second moral horror to the first, to have, and in a far higher degree, the same disqualification."—' Calderón,' by Archbishop Trench, 1880.[1]

NOTE V

" Nor peace within, nor calm around " sang the poet in his stanzas written in dejection near Naples. That the thought of Harriet, suppressed by conscious effort, poisoned the very roots of the poet's soul and contributed to steep with melancholy his more spontaneous lyrics can hardly be doubted. A page from Peacock witnesses to the violent effort which Shelley applied to the suppression of this episode of his life:

> " I was walking with him [Shelley] one evening in Bisham Wood, and we had been talking, in the usual way, of our ordinary subjects, when he suddenly fell into a gloomy reverie. I tried to rouse him out of it, and made some

---

[1] *Cf.* Menéndez y Pelayo: ". . . obra brutal y de extraordinaria crudeza, aún mayor que la que en sí tiene el argumento, que de suyo es antidramático e inmundo." ('Calderón y su Teatro,' Madrid, 1881, Pp. 12–13).

remarks which I thought might make him laugh at his own abstraction. Suddenly he said to me, still with the same gloomy expression, 'There is one thing to which I have decidedly made up my mind. I will take a great glass of ale every night.' I said, laughingly, 'A very good resolution as the result of a melancholy musing.' 'Yes,' he said, 'but you do not know why I take it. I shall do it to deaden my feelings : for I see that those who drink ale have none.' The next day he said to me : 'You must have thought me very unreasonable yesterday evening ?' I said, 'I did, certainly.' 'Then,' he said, 'I would tell you what I would not tell anyone else. I was thinking of Harriet.' I told him, 'I had no idea of such a thing ; it was so long since he had named her. . . .' "

NOTE VI

This scene of " El Mágico Prodigioso " may well have been the " incident " which suggested his dream as related in " Shelley Memorials " (quoted by Peacock, p. 79) :

" One night, loud cries were heard issuing from the saloon. The Williamses rushed out of their room in alarm ; Mrs. Shelley also endeavoured to reach the spot, but fainted at the door. Entering the saloon the Williamses found Shelley staring horribly into the air, and evidently in a trance. They waked him, and he related that a figure wrapped in a mantle came to his bedside and beckoned him. He must then have risen in his sleep, for he followed the imaginary figure into the saloon, when it lifted the hood of its mantle, ejaculated ' Siete sodisfatto ? ' and vanished. The dream is said to have been suggested by an incident occurring in a drama attributed to Calderón."

NOTE VII

Shelley's translation is indeed a striking proof of his insight into Calderón's art and style. Expression is not always crystal-

like in Calderón. He sometimes strains his thought to suit his
images and twists his sentences in order to cage them within
the narrow walls of his versification. But Shelley's ingenuity
in disentangling the sense overcomes all obstacles. At times
the younger poet improves the melody of the original, though,
perhaps, at the expense of the image. Thus:

> . . . When the sun seeks its grave among the billows,
> Which, among dim gray clouds on the horizon
> Dance like white plumes upon a hearse . . .

is a poor if more musical rendering of—

> Cuando el sol cayendo vaya
> A sepultarse en las ondas
> Que entre oscuras nubes pardas
> Al gran cadáver de oro
> Son monumentos de plata.

Shelley's softer melody sometimes affects the thought itself,
which, from a set assertion, expands into a *mood* under the
translator's romantic inspiration. Calderón had *said*—

> . . . Que no hay firme bien debajo
> De los cercos de la luna,

and Shelley *sings*—

> . . . for nothing
> Beneath the circle of the moon but flows
> And changes, and can never know repose.

But in Shelley's hands the original generally loses in strength
what it gains in grace and atmosphere. When Justina triumphs
over the Devil who has tempted her, the vanquished fiend con-
fesses his failure in two lines of admirable energy:

> Venciste, mujer, venciste,
> Con no dejarte vencer.

The hammer-like effect of this phrase is well-nigh untranslatable. Shelley's attempt is very poor :

> Woman, thou hast subdued me,
> Only by not owning thyself subdued.

An exception to this rule, but a brilliant exception, is the passage in which the Devil addresses Cipriano in Jornada II. Here Shelley was in his favourite element. Calderón had brought out the satanic pride of the conquered angel, but Shelley emphasises it most powerfully, even beyond Calderón's own expression. Here is a typical example of Shelley's treatment of the subject :

> Si fueron temeridades
> No me vi en ellas tan solo
> Que de sus mismos vasallos
> No tuviese muchos votos,

becomes—

> Nor was I alone,
> Nor am I now, nor shall I be alone ;
> And there was hope, and there may still be hope,
> For many suffrages among his vassals
> Hailed me their lord and king, and many still
> Are mine, and many more perchance shall be.

ENGLISH SIDELIGHTS ON SPANISH LITERATURE

I

SEVERAL years ago—and I should not like to be pressed
as to the exact number—an old cook in Glasgow was
suddenly informed by the young lady of the house that
she—the young lady—was going to marry a Spaniard.
" Are ye no feared ? " asked the cook. The question was
not in the least unnatural. I remember myself that once
when I was staying in a little town in one of the southern-
most counties of Scotland, there came a company of
players, the best actors in the world either for light or
for heavy opera, for dramatical-comical, comical-senti-
mental, sentimental-dramatical-comical, music-hall un-
musical or variety invariable. They produced a play,
the name of which I have, to my shame, forgotten ; a
masterpiece of that difficult art, the melodrama. The
action took place at sea on board ship, and the most thrill-
ing scene thereof in the Captain's own cabin. This
cabin was remarkable for its simple yet forcible furniture,
which consisted of two pictures hanging on the blank
wall on either side of the only door, and representing
the two most terrifying ruffians ever brushed by a tenth-
rate Goya : two types fascinating indeed for their very
superlativity—if I may coin the word—eyes the most
ferocious, hair the most luxuriant and rebellious, beard
and moustache the blackest and thickest and supply of
arms and ammunition the most formidable and imposing
ever witnessed or imagined. The knot of the play was a

mutiny on board, which the gallant captain negotiated in an admirable scene. He called all the rebellious crew to his cabin, produced a rusty pistol and thundered forth : " Surrender, or I will blow the ship to pieces ! " Then, pointing to the two ruffians on the wall, he added in a flesh-creeping voice : " I have Spanish blood in my veins. *There* are my ancestors ! " The crew filed out like a flock of lambs, and a thrill ran through the audience.

An old nation like Spain could not but return such civility. In a book published in Seville in 1529[1] there is a lengthy and detailed account of a trial before the King of Scotland between

" a lady named Brasayda, one of the wisest in the world for her knowledge and her sprightliness and other qualities appertaining to gracefulness, who, for her great deserts, had been through many a love battle and many a case worthy of record ; and a gentleman from the kingdom of Spain, whose name was Torrellas, a man distinguished for his knowledge of women and very bold in love matters and very witty, as is shown in his works."

Brasayda and Torrellas presented before the King of Scotland the case for and against women. It was one of the many episodes of the old dispute concerning the fairness of the fair sex in which Chaucer took part, though with little conviction, on the side of women. According to the Spanish book, which is not, I confess, very reliable, it was Torrellas, that is the accuser of women, who won the case. But the women of Scotland, headed by their queen, took a prompt and terrible

---

[1] " *Tractado de Grisel y Mirabella, compuesto por Juan de Flores a su amiga,*" Sevilla, Cromberger, 1529. Quoted by Marcelino Menéndez y Pelayo. 'Historia de la Poesía Castellana en la Edad Media,' II, p. 268.

revenge, the description of which I must leave to the Spanish chronicler :

" And he was then stripped of his clothes, and they covered his mouth so that he could not complain, and he was firmly tied to a post, all naked, and there each woman brought a new invention to torture him, and there were some who with burning tongs and other with nails and teeth, furiously tore him to pieces. . . ."

The narrative may be left there since what follows is still worse. But this fragment amply shows that Spain could if necessary build images of Scotland as picturesque as the images which Scotland could build of Spain.

Nor was England less favourably treated by Spanish imagination. Writing in 1482, Mosén Diego de Valera, knight, diplomat, political intriguer and historian in his way, devotes a chapter of his " Corónica de España y Corónica Abreviada " to the description of the Kingdom of England which he calls " a very big island placed in the ocean sea out of the roundness of the world."[1] In this chapter which, like the rest of the book, is addressed to Queen Isabel the Catholic, Mosén Diego inserts the following passage :

" Towards the East, by the seaside, it is asserted by many, there are trees whose leaves, if falling on the sea, become fishes, and those that fall on land become birds of the size of sea-gulls. And in order to ascertain the truth I asked the Lord Cardinal of England, your uncle, brother of the Serenísima Queen Doña Catalina your grandmother ; who assured me that it was so."

[1] " Isla muy gráde situada en el mar oceano : fuera de toda la redó-deza del mundo," perhaps a reminiscence from Vergil :
Et penitus toto divisos orbe Britannos,

One can see the smile of the princely Cardinal float between the lines of this passage. Yet, measured by the standards of that age, in which men's capacity for believing was not hindered by so much concrete knowledge as in ours, Mosén Diego's story is not more wildly fantastic than many a tale about Spain printed in relatively modern English books.

There seems then to be ample scope for the activities of bodies such as the Spanish Society of Scotland and the Anglo-Spanish Society. Though much has been written and said about British insularity, there is little doubt that the British people have in the very complexity of their national composition an excellent basis for the sound knowledge and understanding of European peoples. Few nations in Europe can trace within their boundaries Norwegian and Iberian, French and Teutonic strains of blood. Britain can. As far as Spain is concerned her stock is well represented in the western side of the island by that element of the population which used to be named Keltic and is nowadays considered as predominantly Iberian. We shall be wise not to lay too much stress on these racial connections between peoples living and developing in such distant and different geographical and historical environments, but the unprejudiced observer cannot help being struck by the similarity of type, movements, rhythm and even customs between certain populations of Western Britain and the peoples that inhabit the Northern regions of Spain.

The point has its interest because, whether racial considerations are to guide us or not, we find in English and Spanish literature and history a curious parallelism, not exactly a coincidence, but a parallelism, which suggests common tendencies in the national character of both peoples. There is a Spanish as well as an English insularity. Our land is known as the Peninsula because it touches the main land along the French border. But who doubts that the Pyrenees were and perhaps still are a barrier to European influences as effective as, nay, more effective than, the Channel? Spain is the Island of the South-West. Neither the Reformation nor even the Renaissance succeeded in effecting a landing on her inaccessible shores. The most glorious chapter of her history, and perhaps of all history, was not writ over European lands, but across the Atlantic seas. Like England, Spain, placed at the westernmost end of Europe, turns her back to the Continent and looks towards her own image in the New World. Like England, Spain succeeded in keeping a strong character of her own through centuries of European life and development. Like England, Spain is in Europe, but not of Europe.

II

It is not surprising, therefore, that two peoples so symmetrically placed by nature, as it were in the north-western and in the south-western suburbs of European culture, should evince a certain similarity in their literary development. And that this similarity exists no one will doubt who has cast a glance at both the Spanish and the English literatures. It appears from the beginning in the dominant character of their epic national poetry. Though Beowulf is much older than Mio Cid, a comparison is quite justified between them if only because these two poems constitute the starting-points in the present chronology of English and Spanish literary works. Now, nothing is more striking than the coincidence between English opinion on Beowulf and Spanish opinion on Mio Cid. Thus, Prof. Macneile Dixon says of the first :

" Our pre-Norman literature, like Beowulf, harsh and untutored though it be, is firmly rooted in experience. How clearly it sees life for what it is and how fearlessly meets it ! It faces the world with a philosophy unborrowed from books and yet perfectly suited to that world. Compare Beowulf with Homer, and you may safely claim Homer's superiority in beauty and poetic quality, not so safely his superiority in masculine vigour and truth."[1]

And Prof. W. P. Ker on the same theme :

" The impression left by Beowulf . . . is that of a noble manner of life, of courtesy and freedom, with the dignity of tragedy attending it."[2]

Now listen to Menéndez Pelayo speaking of the " Song of Mio Cid " :

" The lands which our heroes tread are not an unknown and fantastic region, sown over with prodigies and monsters ; they are the same moors and the same hills which we tread and inhabit. This poetry does not dazzle the imagination, but gets hold of it by a certain barbaric majesty due to sheer simplicity and evidence ; to sheer lack of art. . . . But there is [in it] another kind of art, more sublime, which does not know itself, and merging into the divine unconsciousness of natural forces gives us the full vision of reality."[3]

[1] 'Poetry and National Character,' by Professor W. Macneile Dixon, p. 30.
[2] 'English Literature, Medieval,' by Professor W. P. Ker, p. 30.
[3] 'Historia de la Poesía Castellana,' por Marcelino Menéndez y Pelayo Vol. I, p. 128.

Reality. The word is as much at home in England as in Spain. In current English these two words, Realism and Spain, do not seem willingly to mix in one sentence. The word Spain evokes romance, chivalry, gorgeous pageantry, high deeds, pennants and standards, lances and swords moving in the golden hue of a legendary atmosphere ; a glory and a beauty luminous and unreal like those illusions which the English language significantly calls " castles in Spain." But this golden light hovering upon her English name does not irradiate from Spain. It falls on her from the eyes of dreaming Englishmen. It is the glow of remembrance that beautifies and not so much idealises as unrealises the past.

Spain for all that is very real and very realistic. Were we to choose between English and Spanish epics, in this respect, Mio Cid would certainly be more at home in this world than Beowulf. Beowulf is a somewhat vague hero who goes slaying imaginary monsters, and his poet had to fetch him out of the memory of the race, for a new spell of activity on paper. But there is not one single monster in Mio Cid, and supernatural influences are limited to an unimportant and perfectly natural apparition of Gabriel to the sleeping hero—an episode to which neither the hero nor his followers nor even his chronicler seem to grant the slightest importance. Moreover, the hero and the poet are separated by the least possible stretch of time and space, so that in Mio Cid Spanish literature gives its first and striking proof of its ability to make poetry out of the here and now. The geography of the poem has been identified by Señor Menéndez Pidal step by step. The most accurately described episodes take place in the region round Medinaceli, where the poet was probably born. The poem was written about forty years after the death of Rodrigo Diaz whom it immortalised. The incidents told are all possible, plausible, in fact, historical. Yet there is poetry in them, a kind of epic poetry comparable to the greatest written in Europe since the days of Homer.

This capacity for turning an almost immediate reality into poetry is due in the first place to the ethical detachment of the poet ; in the second place to his dramatic genius. His Cid would not be an ever-living hero had the poet limited his size to the possibly narrow dimensions of his own mind. Humble and unprejudiced, guided only by his unfailing æsthetic instinct, the poet set down his hero as he really was : not a slayer of monsters nor a model of knights, perfect to the point of abstraction, but a man, a soldier, a leader of men, an adventurer with all the dust and blood of his earth and his battles on him, a cautious captain, ready to bargain off a dangerous enemy, a shrewd negotiator, and withal, a father, a husband and a genial friend. And we know when he smiled and when he shed tears, and when he crossed himself— and we know also where he camped and where he fed his horses ; and when and why he was generous towards the king who had exiled him, and when and why he obtained a loan from two Jews of Burgos, leaving behind as security two heavy coffers full of sand. In short, a Don Quixote and a Sancho rolled into one, less the touch of madness in the master, and the touch of simplicity in the squire.

He was a real poet who knew how to respect his model so. But he was a great poet who so forcibly rendered characters and scenes. In this ancient monument of Spanish literature the dramatic genius of Spain is already at work. Too often, and particularly in connection with Spain, the word *dramatic* is interpreted as if it meant *theatrical*. Corneille himself was not wholly innocent of this misinterpretation. But the theatrical is to the dramatic what cant is to truth. Dramatic genius aims at the poetical rendering of actions ; theatrical talent is purely concerned with effect. A certain amount of theatrical talent generally goes to the making of great dramatists, as the menial side of their activity ; just as in every sculptor there is a stone-cutter who works for the poet of plastic form. Nor is it possible to draw a sharp line between the lofty and the menial activity in artists since both spring from the same root tendency and their difference lies solely in the intention which directs their movements and colours their results. It will be found of course that in all good drama theatrical ability is kept in its place as the handmaid of dramatic inspiration. In the " Song of Mio Cid," it may even be said that there is not the slightest trace of it. The author is obviously so much impressed with the subject that he states the facts simply, in their order, without condescending to disturb the tranquillity of his narrative with tricks, preparations, or attempts at surprising, suspending or horrifying his readers. He is sure that the story, plainly told, will impress his readers and hearers as deeply as the facts impressed him.

Yet, despite its even development, the " Song of Mio Cid " is written with such dramatic power that in its lines we seem already to hear the language of Lope, Tirso and Calderón. There is, no doubt, an inherent dramatic quality in the Spanish language itself, as there is a philosophic quality in the German and a mathematical quality in the French. The French word defines the idea ; the German word expands it ; the Spanish word presents it. While the German word is fat and roomy like a book, and the French word is thin and clear like a geometric line, the Spanish word is foursquare, like a thing, bare and standing before our eyes. This is no mere philological distinction, but a difference which reminds us that words are but medals of sound stamped by the spirit. German, French, Spanish words bear the particular impress of the spirit of Germany, France, Spain. Thus Spanish words are forcible and dramatic because the language gives back in energy of expression all the spring and eagerness with which the Spanish mind falls upon reality, like an eagle on its prey.

The author of the " Song of Mio Cid " knew how to make use of this virtue of our language. Words, lines, passages, full of dramatic force are too frequent for quotation. His dramatic imagination is so vivid that he often places himself among the spectators and feels the impression of the scene and breaks into an exclamation of wonder, terror or delight.

> Dios, que alegre fo el abbat don Sancho.   243
> Lord, how glad was the abbot don Sancho.

And the details instinctively chosen to render each scene are precisely those which would impress a personal witness of the event and would leave behind the deepest trace. Thus, the arrival of the hero at the monastery of San Pero where his wife Dª Ximena has taken refuge :

> Hurriedly sing the cocks and the dawn wants to break,
> When the good canpeador arrived at San Pero.

The Abbot Don Sancho, a Christian of the Creator
Was praying matins at the turn of dawn
And Doña Ximena, with five ladies of rank
Was praying to St. Peter and the Creator :
" Thou who guidest us all, help My Cid Canpeador."
There was a knock at the door and they heard the message.
Lord, how glad was the Abbot Don Sancho !
With lights and candles they all jumped into the courtyard ;
With so much joy they receive the one who was born in a good
    hour.[1]

How admirably described the contrast between the
peace and silence of the monastery in prayers and the
excitement and turmoil raised by the arrival of the hero.
How homely the detail of the lights and candles, how
true and humble that word *corral*, which sets the scene
on our everyday earth, not in the unreal atmosphere of
books and marvels ; and how deeply epic in its innocence
and unselfconsciousness that appeal to Fate implied in
the last line : *he who was born in a good hour.* For
though supernatural influences are almost wholly lacking
in Mio Cid, the poet is too sincere a realist not to give
to Fate at least that part which men give it in their
thoughts and prejudices. When describing the first

---

[1] Apriessa cantan los gallos e quieren crebar albores,   235
   Cuando llegó a San Pero el buen Canpeador ;
   El abbat don Sancho, cristiano del Criador
   Rezaba los matines a vuelta de los albores.
   Y estaba doña Ximena con çinco dueñas de pro,
   Rogando a San Pero e al Criador.
   "Tu que a todos guias, val a myo Çid el Canpeador."
   Llamaron a la puerta, e sopieron el mandado ;
   Dios, que alegre fo el abbat don Sancho.
   Con lumbres e con candelas al corral dieron salto,
   Con tan grant gozo reciben al que en buen ora nasco.

march of the little band into exile, signs and omens begin
to be noted :

As they went out of Bivar, they had the crow on their right,
As they went into Burgos they had it on their left.[1]

and the reiteration of the " good hour " theme, per-
sistently and deliberately used though with remarkable
variety of form, succeeds in crowning the hero with a
kind of aureole without in the least departing from the
world of tangible reality.

My Cid Roy Diaz, he who girt his sword in a good hour.
Lo, Canpeador, in a good hour thou wert born !
He came towards the tent of him who was born in a good hour.[2]

This blending of reality with Fate, so skilful in its self-
ignorance, is perhaps the crowning feature which makes
Mio Cid the worthy epic of the race and one of the
greatest epic poems of post-classical times.

III

Realism, freedom from ethical prejudice, and dramatic
genius are the three main qualities which assert themselves in Spanish epics. They are also the dominant
features of the most arresting personality in Spanish
medieval literature : Juan Ruiz, probably the most un-

[1] A la exida de Bivar ovieron la corneja diestra
e entrando en Burgos ovieronla siniestra.

[2] Myo Çid Roy Diaz el que en buen ora çinxo espada.   58
Ya, Canpeador, en buen ora fostes naçido !   71
Vino pora la tienda del que en buen ora nasco,   202

worthy archpriest of Hita, yet the only one who achieved immortality. Ticknor, Menéndez y Pelayo and Prof. Fitzmaurice Kelly have compared him to Chaucer. A thoroughly worked-out parallel might prove an exercise of more than merely academic interest, not only on account of the curious likeness, but more especially for the suggestive differences existing between the somewhat elusive Londoner and the genial and perhaps no less elusive Spanish priest.

The first connection between them is the fact that they occupy a similar position in their respective literatures, each of them the chief poet of the fourteenth century—Juan Ruiz in its first, Chaucer in its second half— each of them closing the epic and narrative age and heralding from afar the period of literary splendour which for England as for Spain sets in towards the end of the sixteenth century. But apart from this historical coincidence, Juan Ruiz and Chaucer have many a common feature. Both possess the power of setting the mind in a smiling mood, for both were good-humoured, large-hearted, rich in that understanding which is born of true fraternity. Both, like true great poets, created worlds of their own, and, since they were creators it goes without saying that they were free from bitterness, for no life ever came out of a bitter heart. Hence the delicious taste of their irony, which in the English as in the Spanish master was of that subtle quality, more connected with the heart than with the brain, graphically called in English " laughing in one's sleeve." A fleeting, silent laughter it is, which does not cause the slightest quiver in the rhythm of the poem : witness this delightful line in which Juan Ruiz describes Don Jimio (Sir Monkey) the

mayor and magistrate of Bugía, who hears the case
between the Wolf and the Fox:

> He was subtle and wise, he never sat for nothing.[1]

This line Chaucer might have written. But simi-
larly, the priest who wrote the praise of small women
because, as he says,

> Of evil, take the least, so says the wise man,
> Therefore, of women, the smallest is the best,[2]

would have concurred with Chaucer in this dictum put
in the loquacious mouth of the Wife of Bath:

> For trusteth wel, it is an impossible
> That any clerk wol speke good of wyves.

This is no misogyny—a horrid word for a horrid thing
—but good-humoured and ironical exaggeration. There
is a passage in Juan Ruiz's "Book of Love,"—for the only
book which this laughing satirist has left us bears that
name, and with less irony than one might think—in
which his mischievous spirit reaches the line of cynicism.
It is a passage frequently quoted, and it occurs in the
prose prologue placed immediately after the prayer to
Jesus Christ with which the book opens.

"Chosing and loving with good intention salvation and love
of paradise for my soul, I wrote this small text in memory of
virtue; and I composed this new book in which are written
down several manners and crafts and deceitful subtleties of
foolish worldly love, which some folk will follow in order to
sin. The which reading and hearing, men or women of good

---

[1] Era sotil e sabio, nunca seía de balde
[2] Del mal tomar lo menos, dícelo el sabidor,
Por ende de las mujeres la mejor es la menor.

understanding and mindful of their salvation, will decide and act, and will be able to say with the Psalmist : Viam veritatis, etc.

" Also, those of little understanding will not go astray; for they, reading and bearing in mind the evil they do or mean to do, and the hardened sinners, their evil arts and the public knowledge of their numerous deceitful ways wherewith they sin and deceive women, will consult their memory and will not lightly hold their good name ; for he is very cruel who contemns his own fame ; the law says it. And they will prefer the love of themselves to the love of sin ; for sensible charity begins with our own selves ; so say the Decretals. And they will reject and abhor the evil manners and crafts of worldly love which causes souls to fall and to deserve the wrath of God, impoverishing life and bringing about ill fame and dishonour and many evils to the body. Notwithstanding, as it is human to sin, were there people desirous of following the ways of foolish love (which I do not advise them to do) they would find here several manners of doing it. And thus, this my book, to all men and women, to the wise and to the unwise, to those who understand virtue and choose salvation and behave well in love of God ; also to those who run after worldly love, in the road that each will tread, will be able to say : Intellectum tibi dabo, etc."[1]

[1] Escogiendo e amando con buena voluntad salvación e gloria del paraíso para mi ánima, fiz esta chica escritura en memoria de bien ; e compuse este nuevo libro, en que son escritas algunas maneras e maestrías e sotilezas engañosas del loco amor del mundo, que usan algunos para pecar. Las cuales, leyéndolas e oyéndolas home o mujer de buen entendimiento que se quiera salvar, descogerá, e obrar lo ha ; e podrá decir con el Salmista : *Viam veritatis*, etc.

Otrosí, los de poco entendimiento non se perderán ; ca leyendo e coidando el mal que facen o tienen en la voluntad de facer, e los porfiosos de sus malas maestrías, e descobrimiento publicado de sus muchas engañosas maneras que usan para pecar e engañar las mujeres, acordarán la memoria e non despreciarán su fama ; ca mucho es cruel quien su fama menosprecia : el Derecho lo dice. E querrán mas amar a sí mesmos que al pecado ; que

It was in this very mood that Chaucer wrote the concluding lines in his Miller's Prologue. Of the Miller's tale he says :

> Methinketh that I shal reherce it here. 3170
> And ther-fore every gentil wight I preye,
> For goddes love, demeth nat that I seye
> Of evel entente, but that I moot reherce
> Hir tales alle, be they bettre or werse,
> Or elles falsen som of my matere.
> And therfore, who-so list it nat y-here,
> Turne over the leef, and chese another tale ;
> For he shal finde y-nowe, grete and smale,
> Of storial thing that toucheth gentillesse,
> And eek moralitee and holinesse ;
> Blameth nat me if that ye chese amis.
> The Miller is a cherl, ye knowe wel this ;
> So was the Reve, and othere many mo,
> And harlotrye they tolden bothe two.
> Avyseth yow and putte me out of blame ;
> And eek men shal nat make ernest of game.

This last line is echoed in Juan Ruiz's warning to his reader :

> Do not misunderstand the story of the Daughter of Endrino.
> I told it in order to teach you, not because it happened to me.[1]

la ordenada caridad, de sí mesmo comienza : el Decreto lo dice. E desecharán e aborrecerán las maneras e maestrías malas del loco amor, que face perder las almas e caer en saña de Dios, apocando la vida e dando mala fama e deshonra, e muchos daños a los cuerpos. Empero porque es humanal cosa el pecar, si algunos (lo que non los consejo) quisieren usar del loco amor, aquí fallarán algunas maneras para ello. E ansí este mi libro, a todo home o mujer, al cuerdo e al non cuerdo, al que entendiere el bien e escogiere salvación, e obrare bien amando a Dios ; otrosí al que quisiere el amor loco, en la carrera que andudiere, puede cada uno bien decir : *Intellectum tibi dabo*, etc.

[1] Entiende bien mi hestoria de la fija del Endrino,
Díjela por te dar ensiempro, non porque a mi vino.

It is the sop that the poets give to their moral conscience. That tribute paid to the supremacy of virtue over vice, both Chaucer and Juan Ruiz feel free to follow the changing ways of men and women, the changing human ways which wind through the abstract lines of vice and virtue like rivers through meridians and parallels. And here again we find that unprejudiced, that innocent impartiality in observation which is an indispensable condition of universal and permanent art. Chaucer puts it with admirable lucidity and sincerity in the passage just quoted. " I moot," he says, " reherce Hir tales alle—

> be they bettre or werse,
> Or elles falsen som of my matere."

Here speaks the conscience of the artist holding its own against the conscience of the moralist. The word " FALSEN," and that possessive " My matere," are truly illuminating as to the depth of Chaucer's artistic vocation. Juan Ruiz's vocation was not less deep.

> I, Juan Ruiz, the abovesaid Archpriest of Hita,
> But whose heart cannot leave off writing poetry. . . .[1]

It is this æsthetic impartiality, born of the depth and sincerity of their poetic vocation, which is the secret of their dramatic power. Of all the glorious chain of poets which England gave to the world, Chaucer is perhaps, after Shakespeare, the one endowed with the greatest dramatic genius. There is a close sympathy between Chaucer and Shakespeare, suggested in part by the range of their respective worlds, their choice of

---

[1] Yo, Joan Ruiz, el sobredicho Arcipreste de Hita
Pero que mi corazón de trovar non se quita . . .

subjects and the free yet accurate style of their character drawing. A similar relationship can be established between Juan Ruiz and the great Spanish dramatists of the Golden Century, particularly those who, like Lope de Vega and Tirso de Molina, excelled in the interpretation of life as they saw it under their own eyes. Juan Ruiz is, like them, a born dramatist. Despite his diffuseness, he knows the secret of that direct plunge into action which is typical of Spanish *romances* no less than of Spanish *comedias*, and, nowadays, of popular songs. He often breaks the tale into a dialogue, dropping all the narrative padding and leaving the characters alone to speak the story out of their own mouths. And, in true national fashion, he is wont to refer to the creatures of his own fancy as if they stood there in front of him :

Oh Lord, how beautiful comes Doña Endrina through the square !
What a figure, what a grace, what a tall neck like a heron's !
What hair, what a mouth, what a complexion, what a graceful gait !
With arrows of love she wounds whenever she lifts her eyes ![1]

Notice the rhythm of these lines, no less descriptive than the words, no less suggestive of the graceful gait of the young woman approaching. For we must recognise yet another poetic virtue which links Chaucer and Juan Ruiz and generally Spanish with English poetry in their equal ability to render movements of nature not so much by the elementary method of describing them to the

---

[1] ¡Ay ! ¡Dios, e cuán fermosa viene Doña Endrina por la plaza !
¡Qué talle, qué donaire, qué alto cuello de garza !
¡Qué cabellos, qué boquilla, qué color, qué buena andanza !
Con saetas de amor fiere cuando los sus ojos alza,

intellect as by the subtle use of that eminently poetic faculty which we might call rhythmical intuition. It is a faculty in which the lyrical and the dramatic tendencies meet, and the fact that it should be prominent in Juan Ruiz and in Chaucer is a fit reminder that both the English and the Spanish poets had a lyric string to their lutes. Nor is it less significant that in Juan Ruiz's as in Chaucer's lyrical poetry the Virgin Mary should occupy such a pre-eminent place. In the " Book of Good Love " there are no less than nine poems in praise of the Virgin. But, though there is grace in these lyrical attempts and a certain *naïveté* which, to us, at any rate, tastes as sweet as sincerity itself, it may be said of Juan Ruiz's lyrical poetry exactly what Professor Legouis says of Chaucer's :

" It is in truth but a tiny stream of lyric which skirts the large fields of his narrative production, and it is not by any means the most characteristic nor, curiously enough, the most personal part of his work."[1]

These are coincidences deeper and more numerous than it is usual to find between great poets of different lands. But a comparative study of Chaucer and Juan Ruiz reveals differences, both personal and literary, which are no less striking and suggestive. While endorsing the parallel put forward by Ticknor, Professor Fitzmaurice Kelly qualifies it by adding : " though the Spaniard lacks the dignity of the Englishman." The observation is of course true, and the more remarkable for the fact that dignity is a quality which is usually

[1] Emile Legouis. ' Geoffrey Chaucer,' Translated by L, Lailavoix, p, 61,

ascribed to Spaniards with an almost automatic security. It would seem ungracious to enter a protest against an obviously well-meant preconception. Yet dignity is not one of those qualities which necessarily go to the making of literary genius. For it implies a sense of measure, of moderation, of submission to moral-social laws, of self-restraint; and genius, more often than not, breaks through these half social, half individual fetters, impelled by stronger and more elementary impulses. Thus there are great literary names below dignity—for instance, Rabelais; and there are some above dignity—for instance, Pascal and Dostoievsky. It was owing to their curiously similar sense for " standing by " while the game was being played that Cervantes and Shakespeare managed to develop the full scope of their genius without moving out of the plane of dignity. But Spanish literature is often out of this middle plane : either soaring above it with St. Teresa, or else exploring beneath it with the picaresque novel and Quevedo. Juan Ruiz undoubtedly belongs to this second group. Though we need not believe that he experienced all the adventures which he relates in his book, the mere fact that he should have lent himself his own name and person as an *anima vilis* for his cynical stories would condemn him on that account. We are far, with him, from that decorous London burgess, no doubt fond of merry-making, yet respectable, a civil servant of his time, a regular worker who studiously read and wrote in his silent room after having settled " his reckonings." Chaucer says that his " abstinence is lyte." But the word abstinence betrays his moderation. With Juan Ruiz, abstinence was far out of sight.

The difference in social status and manners between Chaucer and Juan Ruiz could hardly be more instructing. Chaucer is a courtier, a past master in that difficult art of pleasing the powerful; if not a nobleman, a man used to the manners of noblemen, by them respected and protected, and in fact, a part of noble life. Juan Ruiz is a priest of that disorderly type which his time tolerated; his favourite company are the people, and particularly that part of the Spanish population which it is so difficult to imagine nowadays and in which Jews and Moors and Christians mixed in an amiable fraternity of mirth and pleasure. He seems to have considered himself as the poet of that variegated set of Jewish and Moorish dancers, blind beggars, night-adventuring students, vagabonds who go from door to door and old procuresses, of which he obviously was a distinguished member.[1] Juan Ruiz is in fact a bohemian. He has all the recklessness of that picturesque race, and therein lies perhaps the gravest cause of his inferiority to Chaucer. For it is with genius as with all other kinds of wealth that it requires a good administration in order to give a good yield. Chaucer administered his genius with as much accuracy as his tedious official duties of Comptroller of the Wool Customs (probably with *more*). Juan Ruiz squandered it, with truly bohemian unconcern for anything

---

[1] Despues fice muchas cantigas de danza e troteras   1513
   Para judías e moras e para entendederas;
   Para en instrumentos de comunales maneras:
   El cantar que non sabes óilo a cantaderas.
   Cantares fiz algunos de los que dicen los ciegos
   E para escolares que andan nocherniegos,
   E para muchos otros por puertas andariegos
   Cazurros e de bulras, non cabrían en diez priegos.

but the fruits of the hour. Yet it would be unfair to leave this feature of his character at its purely negative estimate. That there was in Juan Ruiz the noble reck-lessness of the loftiest type of Spaniard, no one can doubt after reading the lines in which he forbids anyone to sell or let on hire copies of his book of " Good Love " :

Since it is of Good Love, lend it willingly.
Do not belie its name, nor give it grudgingly.
Do not give it for money, whether for sale or for hire,
For there is no will nor grace nor good love that bought can be.[1]

Chaucer was too sedate, too quiet a *bourgeois* to think in terms of such generous recklessness. He was, on the other hand, more refined and, as Professor Legouis has admirably shown, with a refinement traceable to the French side of his nature, even in his purely English work. Juan Ruiz knew French and read the French poets. Of that there is no doubt. But while Chaucer finds in his English composition enough Norman elements to as-similate the French spirit of poetry almost as a matter of course, Juan Ruiz already evinces that peculiar refrac-toriness of the Spanish race towards the acceptance of any French influence deeper than mere moulds, forms and stock scenes or sentences. France gives to Chaucer not merely a great subject and many a minor tale, but a style, a manner, an attitude, elegance of mind and clearness of diction. From Chaucer onwards, English poetry will never again be wholly un-French. To Juan Ruiz, France gives nothing but the raw matter of some

---

[1] Pues es de buen amor, emprestadlo de grado.
Non desmintades su nombre, nin dedes refertado.
Non le dedes por dineros vendido nin alquilado,
Ca non ha grado nin gracias nin buen amor complado.

risky *fabliaux*. He made of them a thing absolutely his own. Thus we find Juan Ruiz to be the first great example—unless the " Song of Mio Cid " be considered, as well it may, an earlier one—of the tenacity of Spanish genius in its resistance to French influence. A successful influence of France over Spain is only possible in periods of national depression. The greater the Spaniard, the lesser the action of the French mind over him. The statement of this fact is a mere recognition of the difference between the spirit of France and the spirit of Spain. The one goes through the other like a ray of light through a flame—and leaves no trace. In its positive side, this Spanish tenacity guarantees the subsistence of the national genius, more careless and primitive, less conscious of its powers, than its formidable and beautiful neighbour. In its negative side it detracts from the universal value of the genius of Spain. For it may be safely said that, in Europe, at least, the universal value of a culture is in a sense proportional to the amount of French essence which it contains.

The English genius, however, more complex than the Spanish, can be more easily attuned to the influence of France. More conscious, it can also undergo its action without fear of complete absorption. That is why in England a period of French influence need not be, as it is generally in Spain, blighting for the garden of national culture. A French word is never a real alien in a page of English, and it was still less so in Chaucer's time. Thus Chaucer, refined by France, a careful and persevering *bourgeois*, is the superior of Juan Ruiz the bohemian both in quantity and in quality of work. His work has over that of Juan Ruiz that inestimable quality which

Alfred de Vigny described in an immortal line. It is an
œuvre
  " Empreinte du parfum des douces solitudes."

There is not enough solitude in Juan Ruiz's work.
When he sits down to write his head is still humming
with the noise of voices, " instrumentos e todas juglerías."
Hence the shade of difference between his dramatic
genius and that of his English brother poet. Chaucer's
dramatic genius is more thoughtful ; Juan Ruiz's more
active. Chaucer is one degree further removed from the
actual turmoil of life than Juan Ruiz. Chaucer is almost
a painter. Juan Ruiz almost an actor. The most striking
example of this difference is perhaps to be found in their
allegorical work. Chaucer's allegories are pictures. Juan
Ruiz already shows in his that genius for dramatising
abstractions which is going to culminate three centuries
later in the Autos of Calderón.

IV

From Chaucer and Juan Ruiz to Shakespeare and Lope
the transition would be easy were it possible to resist the
temptation to connect the names of Sir Philip Sidney
and Garcilaso de la Vega. Both were noblemen, soldiers,
poets of exquisite refinement, singers of unhappy love ;
both died in the prime of age, Sir Philip at thirty-two,
Garcilaso at thirty-three, both from wounds received in
battle, Sir Philip in 1586, Garcilaso exactly fifty years
earlier. Garcilaso is one of the greatest lyrical poets of
Spain, and as a poet he is certainly superior to Sir Philip
Sidney. He is endowed with a gift relatively rare in
Spanish letters, a certain tenderness, almost feminine,

which gives emotion to his poetry and contributes also
—along with his technical skill—to the fluidity of his
form. Though a reformer and the adapter of Italian
hendecasyllabics to Spanish requirements, he writes a
smooth liquid verse admirably suited for his peaceable,
pastoral scenery, his delicate atmosphere and his melancholy but not desperate tone—precisely that tone in
which Sir Philip Sidney complained, without despairing,
of his unhappy love. His poetry is deliciously fresh,
murmuring and rumorous with the waters of brooks and
rivers and lakes as no other Spanish poetry is, a fact no
doubt related to his stay as a prisoner in the Grosse
Schüt Island on the Danube. His music is as fine as any
written before or since in Spain, a music in fact of a more
subdued and subtle character than the Spanish language
usually yields. He is essentially, not merely in his mind
but in his subjects, an aristocratic poet, such as would
naturally take his place in the English Parnassus, until
quite recently the most exclusive literary club in the
world. In the name of an unenlightened nationalism he
has been accused of lack of " hispanism " because of his
infatuation for the then new Italian forms which his
brilliant example did so much to establish in Spain. The
accusation is on the face of it absurd. Yet there is a
sound though misdirected instinct that considers him as
somewhat un-Spanish. He represents a type of poet
which is not wholly in harmony with the genius of the
race : a refined poet, a sure artist, an exquisite musician.
In Spanish letters he is a great name—but a name apart.

V

We come back to the main stream of both English and Spanish literatures when we contemplate this most striking of literary parallels : the simultaneous growth, splendour and decadence of the Elizabethan and the Spanish Golden Century Theatres. England and Spain are the only two modern nations that can claim to have created a truly original theatre—a theatre come to life by the union of reality and national genius without the intervention of any classical model, prejudice or tradition. This fact in itself should suffice to justify the comparative study of English and Spanish literature as an indispensable complement to the knowledge of each one of them. But how much more imperative such a comparative study will appear when it is realised that those two sole original dramatic creations of modern Europe strongly resemble each other, despite the fact that—at least in so far as Shakespeare and the Spanish masters are concerned —they developed in complete ignorance of one another like two plants of the same seed born in distant lands. Such similarity ought to have imposed long ago the study of Spanish in England and the study of English in Spain as an indispensable element of national culture. For surely there is some deep and as yet almost unexplored relationship between the two peoples who from the extreme north-west and the extreme south-west of the Continent could bring to European culture two offerings so original and so strikingly alike.

The likeness is not limited to that robust and almost barbaric spontaneity with which the English and the Spanish theatres push forth their uncouth vigorous shapes into the polite world ruled by the three unities. It extends to the appetite for action which fills the English as well as the Spanish stage with the movement of living bodies, men and women, and not merely literary exercises. No messengers coming to relate the storm, the battle, the duel, but the duel, the battle and the storm actually taking place on the stage. And faithfully following the wayward ways of nature, clown and hero mingle on the stage, weaving before the audience the ever-mixed cloth of life. Form, in its turn, claims the freedom of rhythm which events themselves impose. In contrast with the French Alexandrine couplet, dragging along the pseudo-classical tragedy at the regular pace of its two yoked oxen, the Spanish and the English dramatists allow themselves the greatest variety of metre. In the Spanish theatre, the romance, that is the sixteen-syllable line assonanced on the same vowels for long stretches of verse, is the basis of versification. It plays in the music of the Spanish theatre a rôle not unlike that of the bag-pipe drone in Scotch national airs. Nor can its discontinuance when other types are employed be raised against this comparison, for its regular beat seems to prolong itself in an undertone through the passages of more lyrical variety. For more menial uses of speech, like letters, announcements and short messages, the Spanish, like the English, theatre falls back into prose. This bold alternance of prose and verse and changeable metre, as also the frequent use of songs and music, creates an atmosphere of vivacity, variety and movement in strong contrast with the somewhat cold decorum of the French tragedy.

Though the founder of the Spanish theatre, and by

far its greatest figure, Lope de Vega had to wait until quite recently before posterity accorded him the fame which he deservedly enjoyed in his lifetime. Calderón, better known, preceded him into European renown. This fact explains why Calderón, believed to be the " central figure " of the Spanish theatre,[1] should have been selected as the prototype with whom to compare Shakespeare. But in actual fact, the real Spanish equivalent to Shakespeare is Lope de Vega. Not only were they both the founders of their national theatres, but they were both of that spontaneous type of genius which most reminds us of the simplicity, fatality and almost awe-inspiring power of natural forces. Of nature, indeed, Shakespeare and Lope have the fecundity and the reckless extravagance and a calm disregard for mere polish, refinement and perfection. When they, as they often do, give us a rendering of apt and felicitous accuracy, we feel that we owe it, not to any painstaking effort of conscientious artistry but to that intuition which their genius gains in the all-pervading sympathy of their outlook. And like all fertile sources of creation, they both inspire in us a mysterious feeling of affection and gratitude, such as we feel for the sea or the earth or the life-giving sun.

Yet the parallel between Lope and Shakespeare cannot be carried much further without having to note down differences which curiously resemble the differences between Chaucer and Juan Ruiz. Lope's marvellous fecundity implied a facility of imagination, construction and execution as favourable to the quantity as harmful to the quality of his work. In the circumstances in which he wrote, his standard of quality is indeed incredibly

[1] Archbishop Trench,

high. His adventurous life did not leave him time enough to deepen and mature his philosophy of life, and of him, no less than of Juan Ruiz, it may be said that, compared to his English brother-spirit, he is inferior in that he failed to cultivate his mind in solitude. Little as we know of Shakespeare's life, he could hardly have grown some of the more complex flowers of his poetry without leisure and tranquillity. Thus it is that Shakespeare deepens into thought and erects a theatre of emotions in the very chambers of the human soul, while Lope spreads out into action and builds a theatre of situations in the open space of tangible reality.

VI

It is not because they were exactly contemporaries, nor in order to complete in an almost childish design the parallel between Lope and Shakespeare, that a similar comparison is here sketched between Milton and Calderón. There is a good basis for it in the somewhat equivalent position which they occupy with regard to the literature of their respective countries, in the wake of a great age, both, in the words of the French poet,

Arrivés trop tard dans un monde trop vieux.

This circumstance links them to each other as the heirs of a literary wealth which gives them a *class* and therefore makes them self-conscious. Gone, that spontaneity of Shakespeare and Lope de Vega, that recklessness, that free flow of inspiration. Milton and Calderón are conscious and conscientious. They know the art of laying out plans, and though rich in genuine inspiration, they seldom allow their muse to dance to any tune but that which suits their own designs.

It is true that Milton is not, strictly speaking, a dramatist, while Calderón was predominantly a playwright. Yet it is impossible to read " Samson Agonistes " without coming to the conclusion that Milton would have been a worthy rival of Shakespeare had he lived fifty years earlier. Given his moral environment, Milton did as much dramatic work as could be expected from him, so that, when analysed, his genius will be found to contain, though perhaps in different proportions, the same literary essences as that of Calderón : the dramatical, the lyrical and the didactical.

For Calderón is perhaps the most lyrical of Spanish dramatists, and his poetry has, like Milton's, the string of bronze as well as the silver string. Led by his lyrical tendency, he not infrequently sacrifices the dramatic to the musical effect, and holds up the action so that the dialogue may acquire the symmetry of an Italian opera duet or *terceto*. The iteration of set sentences as a kind of *leitmotiv* which Tirso de Molina had so gracefully and discreetly used to the enhancement of the dramatic interest, as for instance in " El Burlador de Sevilla," develops, in Calderón, into a complicated exercise of composition almost intolerably mechanical and certainly undramatic. For though Calderón had Milton's conscious artistry, he was not protected in its use by Milton's unfailing taste, and in his regard for form he often lets his thought lose its way in the maze of elaborate labyrinths of style.

This failing, however, is only too natural in a poet who had to write much and to please a difficult public, spoilt by several decades of overflowing dramatic production. In spite of it, Calderón's lyrical flights suggest Milton's own manner, and the resemblance is further strengthened by their common taste for religious and biblical subjects, which they both treat with a stern austerity in deep contrast with the smiling worldliness of Lope de Vega and Shakespeare. But here the specific difference between them is rather the substance than the form of their work. Milton is *the* Protestant Poet, Calderón *the* Catholic Poet *par excellence*. Milton is primarily concerned with character and conduct, while Calderón lays main stress on faith and divine grace. This aspect of Calderón's mind makes him the type of transition from the popular and realistic poets like Lope and Juan Ruiz to the mystic and spiritual poets such as St. Teresa. Realism and mysticism are the two poles of the Spanish mind ; a realism which has something mystic in the intensity of its contemplation and a mysticism which is in love with reality as only those who see God in all things can be. Velázquez and El Greco represent these two tendencies in Spanish painting. Calderón stands midway between the two, or rather reaches both ends, following Velazquez in the clear realism of *The Mayor of Zalamea* and painting his *Life's a Dream* with the violent colours and tortured lines of El Greco.[1]

VII

Leaving aside the crowd of lesser lights, this review of some of the greatest creators in Spanish literature, seen in contrast with their nearest English equivalents, shows

[1] See p. 33.

how consistently the Spanish national genius develops when left to grow under favourable historical conditions. An eager realism is the key-faculty of the race, the cause both of the main quality and of the main defect of its literature. For, under the action of this kind of appetite for reality, the poet can grow flowers of poetry out of the very soil he treads and the very air he breathes; but, meanwhile, the man in him, animated by the same appetite, will tend to spread his life-activities into the world of action and his work will therefore lack that cream of thought which accumulates in tranquil solitude. This realistic element is the vivifying element in Spanish dramatic genius, a literary faculty which Spain possesses to a degree equalled only—not by England—but by the solitary genius of Shakespeare. It also explains the ethical detachment of the Spanish artist which is at bottom a manifestation of his undivided love of reality. In the name of this love no man-made law or prejudice is allowed to check the free flow of life animated by beauty. Beauty is grace of earthly inspiration, that is, the spiritual radiance with which reality appears to the æsthetic mind. But there is a kind of realist, eager more even than the artist, to whom reality appears clothed in radiance of divine grace : this higher realist is the mystic.

Thus, Spanish realists and Spanish mystics are impelled by the same tendency, though in different forms. In the same eager, direct manner in which the one falls on tangible life the other is lifted towards spiritual life and union with God. The greatest and most typically Spanish of our mystics, St. Teresa, writes a marvellous style of her own, which rushes from her heart right into the light of day, impatiently bursting the cumbersome meshes of grammar, order and even logical sense. Dramatic ? This style is more than dramatic ; it is alive and panting ; it is life itself. The anonymous poet who wrote Mio Cid, Juan Ruiz, Lope de Vega, in spite of their directness, sobriety and realistic truth, sound artificial and insincere by the side of its transcendent realism. With her we are as high as the genius of Spain will ever carry us. It is a height beyond art and poetry, in that reality which, like light itself, we cannot see.

SPANISH POPULAR POETRY

NOTE ON BIBLIOGRAPHY

Most of the songs quoted in this work can be found either in Señor Rodríguez Marín's book or in Señor Alonso Cortés' article as mentioned below, and though I had heard many of their coplas before I read them in their works, I could hardly have attempted this essay had I not had at my disposal the invaluable store which they put together with so much patience and industry. The Asturian song quoted, p. 111, is, I believe, unpublished.

CANTOS POPULARES DE CASTILLA, recogidos por Narciso Alonso Cortés. Revue Hispanique. Oct. and Dec., 1914.

CANTOS POPULARES ESPAÑOLES, by Francisco Rodríguez Marín. 5 Vols. 1882.

CANCIONERO POPULAR. Colección escogida de coplas y seguidillas recogidas y ordenadas por D. Emilio Lafuente y Alcántara. Madrid. Bailly-Bailliere. 2 Vols. 1866.

POESÍAS POPULARES colegidas por D. Tomás Segarra, español nativo, profesor de su lengua materna en el Real Instituto el Maximilianum y lector de la Universidad de Munique (Baviera). Leipzig. F. A. Brockhaus. 1 Vol. 1862.

CUENTOS Y POESÍAS POPULARES ANDALUCES coleccionados por Fernán Caballero. 1 Vol. Sevilla. 1859.

COLECCIÓN DE LAS MEJORES COPLAS de seguidillas, tiranas y polos que se han compuesto para cantar a la guitarra, por D. PRECISO. Madrid. Ibarra. 1805. 2 Vols.

NOTE ON TRANSLATION

Translating poetry is a difficult task in the most favourable circumstances. Translating popular poetry, and into a language, though fairly familiar, foreign to the translator, is an almost impossible achievement. The examples given must be taken as mere *approximations* rather than faithful renderings of the original songs. The rule has been to translate above all the mood, then the rhythm and the metrical arrangements, if possible. When the form of the copla had to be changed, and that has been often the case on account of the shorter average length of English words as compared with Spanish words, the song was recast in translation into a metre roughly corresponding to a different popular measure requiring a lesser number of syllables. Thus, often, *cuartetas* are translated into *seguidillas*. But even this at times failed.

Several of the coplas quoted have been spelt, in a roughly phonetic fashion, according to the popular pronunciation prevalent in the South of Spain. The adoption of a regular spelling would have in some cases destroyed the metre and in all cases deprived the copla of its popular flavour.

The pronunciation thus recorded is practically that of the Andalusian dialect. The main changes from the Castilian are the following :—

1. Elision of *e*.
    (*a*) When final before initial vowel sound.
        M'he for *Me he* (p. 123).
    (*b*) Initial, as in *en*.
        está'n for *está en* (p. 99).
2. Fall of *r*.
    (*a*) Final, as in
        flô for *flor* (p. 119).
        vê for *ver* (p. 101).
    (*b*) Intermediate, as in
        ace'a for *acera* (p. 92).
3. Fall of *l* final, as in
        arbo' for *árbol* (p. 116).
4. Fall of *s* final, as in
        metía for *metidas* (p. 120).
5. Fall of *n* final, particularly when followed by *en*.
        pique'n for *piquen en* (p. 120).
6. Fall of *d*.
    (*a*) In endings *ado, ido, ida*.
        buscao for *buscado* (p. 123).
        vestío for *vestido* (p. 104).
        metía for *metidas* (p. 120).
    (*b*) In the preposition *de*, generally accompanied with elision of the remaining *e* and therefore complete disappearance of the word.
        l'ace'a 'enfrente for *la acera de enfrente* (p. 92).
    (*c*) In *donde* (initial *d*) with the elision of *o* after a strong vowel.
        está'nde for *está donde* (p. 99).
    (*d*) In weak positions between two strong vowels.
        tôo for *todo* (p. 113).
        naita for *nadita* (p. 101).
        tôitas for *toditas* (p. 120).

In this last case the hiatus resulting from the fall of the *d* is, according to a well-known rule of Spanish phonetics, transformed into a diphthong by the shifting of the tonic accent to *ó* from *í*. Notice that this does not take place in the case of *naita*, probably because the diphthong is much more energetic than the hiatus, and the mood of the respective coplas is energetic in one case, plaintive in the other. It is an interesting case of psychological influence over phonetics.

7.   *l* becomes *r*, *ar* for *al* (p. 119).
        ll ,, *y*, *barquiyo* for *barquillo* (p. 101).
        z ,, *s*, *rosa* for *roza* (p. 104).
        hue ,, *güe*, *güesos* for *huesos* (p. 104).
        h ,, *j*, *jasta* for *hasta* (p. 104).
8. Several words take a peculiar form,
        náide for *nadie* (p. 123).
        asín for *así* (p. 119).
        arretiré for *retiré* (p. 119).

I

WHEN we approach a work of foreign literature our expectation is twofold. A new beauty is going to be revealed to our artistic sense; a new truth is going to add its light to the truth we know. We are promised the enjoyment of an artistic pleasure, but we are also led to the discovery of human ways, new to us, yet deeply connected with our own ways by similarity, contrast, or, more suggestively still, by delicate shades of difference. Thus, works of foreign literature may be considered under two different aspects; as pure æsthetic *ends*, or works of art; and as *means*, roads of approach to the character of the nation which created them.

It is, indeed, in relation to national character that the study of foreign literature is most illuminating, and, if there are such things as foreign literatures, it is less to the multiplicity of languages than to the multiplicity of national characters that we owe them—witness the differences between American and English, Swiss and German, Spanish and Spanish-American literatures. A national character may be defined as a set of tendencies determined by the relative strength of the tendencies which compose it. All tendencies are in all men, and that is the basis of human unity and solidarity. It cannot be said that one people is intelligent and another one is not; that one lacks imagination and another one moral sense. All peoples possess all the elementary essences of human nature; but all peoples do not possess them in equal proportions. Hence national character. For a difference in quality is but a synthesis of quantitative differences.

In each country, a certain group of tendencies predominates, which gives the key to the character of the nation. Thus, what is specific in France is the predominance of the intellect over all the other faculties. Logic, measure, order, clearness, are the French qualities *par excellence*. The nature of Spain is strongest both below and above the intellectual level: in instinct and in vision, in passion and in mysticism. England's healthy and robust vitality is the main feature of her character and civilisation. It accounts for the strength of her bodily tendencies, mainly observable in the individual, and for the vigour and effectiveness of her social morality, rooted in the depths of her tribal instinct.

These differences in character reveal themselves in the social atmosphere. The intellect is man's *bourgeois* faculty: careful, orderly, hard-working, methodical, pitilessly accurate, tinged with a touch of Voltairian flippancy, revolutionary in theory, but conservative in practice. Thus, France, the country of the intellect, is also a *bourgeois* country. The tone of its society is middle class. Its virtues, its vices, its prejudices, its ideas, politics, economics and the arts are all grounded on a *bourgeois* conception of life. Its theatre, for instance, depicts the habits, preaches the ideas and analyses the passions of its *bourgeoisie*; and every Frenchman, whether a nobleman, a commoner, a peasant, or a proletarian, is in his heart a *bourgeois*, weighted with sound common sense and led by sharp intellect.

The English ideal is aristocratic. The aristocrat is the

highest type of individual which any social organisation can evolve—the human being whose life is richest in those physical values so much prized by every Englishman—cleanliness, light, and air, comfort, leisure, free space on earth, privacy, elegance. He is, moreover, the prototype of the moral-social qualities of the race : a model of character, a standard of self-control, an ideal of reserve, a mirror of gentlemanliness, the very definition of *exclusiveness*. The aristocracy still lives in England, not only because it has always been more active and more socially useful than in other countries, but also because it has and always had the respect, affection and even admiration of the people.[1] And, though the landed and historical aristocracy may die out, the English people will not live without a class in whom to satisfy their national craving for social hero-worship. As the result of the spread of public education, we are already seeing the growth of a new aristocracy based on " culture " and mainly formed of actors, playwrights, and novelists. The English theatre—particularly in its more popular and genuine form, the music-hall—moves in the aristocratic *milieu*, or adopts its ways and mimics its life. Its women wear low necks and long trains ; its men display front shirts and tail coats. The gallery may think this or that about the " idle classes," but when they pay for

[1] I recently had an opportunity to observe how deep and genuine still is the love of English people for their aristocracy. I happened to be in a suburban train when several fellow-passengers began to comment on the death of Lord Brassey, announced in that morning's papers. Someone remarked that he left no heirs, and that, therefore, the title would lapse. "What a pity !" said another passenger. There was not the slightest trace of irony in his voice and manner, and the remark met with general assent.

their ticket they want to see ladies and gentlemen moving about on polished floors.

In deep contrast with the English stage, the Spanish stage—particularly in its most genuine form, the *género chico*—is predominantly popular. Its heroes and heroines are workmen, peasants, the gardener's daughter, the cobbler's wife, the schoolmaster's boy. A ZARZUELA,[1] much admired by Saint-Saëns, has for its heroine a domestic servant. The Spanish people, far from shaping its life on a middle class or aristocratic model, goes its own way with all the independence of taste and conduct to be expected from a class that feels within itself its own ideal. And it can even be observed that the middle and upper classes, instead of being imitated by the people, not infrequently follow the people in its ways of living, thinking, talking, and even in the matter of dress. This is particularly so when some artistic effect is in view, as in the VERBENAS or the FERIAS of Andalucía. The reason is that the people are the most representative class of the Spanish race, a fact that might be anticipated since the Spanish specific qualities are more particularly related to the instincts and the spirit, and are, therefore, essentially popular.

II

It follows that a study of Spanish popular poetry is an excellent way of approach to the knowledge of the Spanish nature, and on this utilitarian ground would amply justify itself. But, truly Spanish in its generosity, our popular poetry will not be content with utility. Useful to the student of human nature, it reveals itself

[1] A kind of small opera.

as eminently pleasant to the lover of beauty. The innumerable songs or COPLAS stored in the living archives of the people's memory form in the aggregate a lyrical poem of such scope, life and beauty as to secure for the Spanish people a place among the great poets of the world. Whether we understand the word " poet " in its restricted sense, meaning by it a craftsman who makes poems as a painter pictures or a jeweller jewels ; or whether, more widely and perhaps more vaguely, we define the poet as a philosopher who contemplates life in an æsthetic attitude, the Spanish people is a great poet. Its poetry is not a mere play of fancy, nor a self-imposed task of culture, nor again a showy mental garment fit for Sunday wear, but a living stream which runs along the road of life and keeps company to the traveller with its murmur and light. The Spaniard *sings*. The mere saying of verse, he considers as an affectation—as, no doubt, it is for all who do not hear the song that is in every true poem. His songs or coplas have a light body —two, three or four lines—that the wings of music may easily lift them. And the popular song takes its flight at every moment and in every place of life—work and rest, field and town, pleasure party or religious procession.

For since every moment of Spanish life yields its own lyrical blossom, religious ceremonies—in Spain, events of public and popular life—could not remain barren. The SAETA—the name itself, *saeta, arrow*, is a poem—is a popular song which any soul in the crowd can sing while the procession is passing through the streets. From the crowd in the street, from the dark recess of a yawning window in a private house, or, may be, from behind the bars of the prison, a voice will suddenly rise ; the holy

image is then turned towards the voice, in a listening
attitude, and the saeta shoots across the intense silence,
like an arrow of poetry. It is difficult to imagine anything more poetical than this custom, or a more striking
proof of the fact that poetry in Spain is an essential
element of everyday life. Yet the saeta is not the most
typical form of Spanish religious poetry. Its subject is
generally of a purely lyrical nature, and its tone is plaintive. It is a lament which an unhappy soul addresses to
its favourite saint or advocation of Christ or the Virgin,
asking for help and comfort, and is nearly always inspired
by some direct personal grief. More typical of Spanish
religious poetry is the plain copla when, flying as it does
over the whole field of life, it happens to alight on a
religious subject. The religious copla is a scene, fresh,
simple, *naïve*, full of light and movement, which by virtue
of the artistic genius of the race brings back to the world
of meadows, rivers and forests the sacred mythology
which books and theologians exiled to heaven. Thus—

> María lava pañales
> Y los tiende en el romero,
> Y los pajaritos cantan
> Y el agua se va riendo.

> Mary is washing baby's linen
> And spreading it on the lavender,
> And the little birds are singing
> And the water runs a-laughing.[1]

This is Spanish. It brings back to Earth and to the
present the vague and the past. It does not seek the

---

[1] See note on spelling and translation, pp. 84, 85.

religious emotion direct, but gives the facts plainly and humbly, and by sheer divination puts again the Holy Family in its real environment, as the family of the carpenter round the corner ; it presents the Virgin Mary at one of the humblest moments of a mother's life, washing the clothes of her infant in the water that " se va riendo " ; and yet, by sheer humility before the facts, a religious emotion is attained, as by the mere contemplation of a quiet and uneventful afternoon. A divine odour of sanctity floats in the clear air of this pure song. Its realism is so intense that it becomes almost mystic, as if those plain, virginal words were the original and secret names of things and actions. And when we reach the last, admirable line, we find it quite natural that the water should run away laughing, with a laughter which is more than the mere murmur of the stream, and is enlivened and deepened by the joy of things that feel the breath of eternal love.

III

We recognise the first and most important poetical quality of the race in this clear gaze of the popular muse, falling over fields and woods, towns and villages, and human nature, with the sharpness and intensity of the Spanish sun and moonlight. It is the clear pictorial gaze of Velázquez. The popular copla becomes a poem by merely expressing things *seen* in street and field and village square, so true it is that a thing well seen is a work of art—

> Tu te vas por l'ace'a 'enfrente,
> Aborreciendo la vida
> Y apeteciendo la muerte.

Sale de la alcoba,
Coloradita como una amapola.

El andar de la madre
Lleva la hija ;
Por pisar menudito
Va tarde a misa.

You seek the other side of the street,
Hating life
And hungry of death.

She comes out of the bedroom
Like a poppy, blushing red.

'Tis the gait of the mother,
The daughter's gait.
She walks with steps so little
At church she's late.

These are the scenes of everyday life, keenly observed
and accurately rendered. The coplas quoted are fair
examples of the direct, concrete, immediate character of
Spanish popular poetry.

For in its popular lyrics no less than in its epics or in
its theatre, classical or contemporary, the Spanish people
give striking proofs of their capacity for making poetry
out of the very life that surrounds them. Usually men
write poetry under the inspiration of one or other of the
two grey muses, Memory and Nostalgia. But neither the
mist of distance nor the mist of time are necessary in
order to make reality poetical in the eyes of the Spanish
people. They love reality so intensely that it yields to
them without resistance like a young and vigorous bride
in whose very vigour and youth lies the weakness that

delivers her into the arms of her lover. Many coplas are little more than simple acts of union between external reality and the mind of the people, small poems of purely æsthetical emotion such as one would feel letting one's hand rest on a shoulder modelled by Michael Angelo or one's eyes on a face painted by Ribera.

> Cuando va andando
> Rosas y lirios va derramando.

> A la entradita del pueblo
> Me alabaron tu hermosura.
> Ojos negros, cara blanca,
> Delgadita de cintura.

> Ayer tarde la vi yo.
> ¡ Ay, galán, si tú la vieras !
> Asomada a la ventana,
> Regando las azucenas.

> Un jardín lleno de nieve
> Parece tu blanco rostro,
> Con tres flores sin cubrir
> Que son tu boca y tus ojos.

When she goes walking
Roses and lilies she goes pouring.

I heard the praise of your beauty
At the village gates,
Your black eyes and your white face
And your slender waist.

I did see her yesterday.
Oh, my friend, if you had seen her !
At her window she was standing,
Watering her lilies,

Your white face is like a garden
Which under snow lies,
And in it three flowers uncovered
Your mouth and your eyes.

This pictorial aspect of Spanish popular poetry may be particularly observed in the CANTAR DE RONDA. The RONDA is a singing party. A small band of young men of the village start in the still of night, well provided with guitars, and walk through the village, stopping to sing under the windows of their present, past or future sweethearts, and generally succeeding in rousing them out of their sleep and making them come to the window to hear the music. There is a copla, which can be heard in Castilian villages, to the effect that—

La noche clara y serena	A night clear and serene
Es buena para rondar.	Is best for a singing party.
Para los enamorados	But for lovers is much better
Es mejor la oscuridad.	A night well covered by darkness.

And whatever we may think of the mischievous ending of this song, the cantar de ronda plainly shows that it was born under the clear light of the moon which cuts out the black squares of the windows on the white walls and brings out in sharp relief the rows and grooves of the tiled roofs. The strong impress of the moonlit roofs on the imagination of the popular *rondadores* appears in such coplas as the following :

Las tejas de tu tejado,
Las flores de tu jardín,
La hermosura de tu cara
Tienen que ser para mí.

Las tejas de tu tejado
Me quieren bajar á abrir.
Baja tú, rosa temprana,
Nacida en el mes de Abril.

The tiles of your roof,
The flowers of your garden,
The beauty of your face
Must belong to me.

The tiles of your roof are wanting
To open the door for me.
Come down yourself, early rose
In the month of April born.

These little poems are *seen* with all the intensity of a painter-poet. But intensity of vision is of no avail without intensity of expression. And it is here that we have to note the admirable energy and conciseness of the Spanish language, both an effect and a condition of the dramatic genius of the race. Within the minute limits of its stage of two, three, or four lines, every one of these songs is a miniature play. The dramatic condensation of some of the coplas is a source of wonder even for the initiated. All the dramatic instinct of the *comedia* and of the *romance* can be found, if anything still more concentrated, in these popular poems, worthy songs of the people of Mio Cid and Lope de Vega.

Here is a drama of sudden love, in three lines, the intensity of which rests almost wholly on the extraordinary strength which the word *madre* has in the Spanish language—

Mira tú si es cosa grande.
La conocí el otro día,
La quiero más que a mi madre.

Think what a strange thing that is.
I knew her but the other day.
I love her more than my mother.

Here is a novel in four lines :

Me quisiste, me olvidaste,
Por la ambición del dinero.
Con las lágrimas regabas
Los trajes de terciopelo.

You loved me once ; you forgot me,
For the love of wealth.
With your tears you have watered
Many a velvet dress.

Here is a graceful epigram :

Dices que no la quieres
Ni vas a verla,
Pero la veredita
No cría yerba.

You say you do not love her,
Nor go to see her ;
Yet no grass ever grows
Over her path.

Here is excellent comedy :

A tu madre se lo dije ;
A tu padre no me atrevo.
En sabiéndolo tu madre
Tu padre lo sabrá luego.

I have told your mother ;
Your father, I dare not.
As your mother knows it,
Your father will soon know.

And lastly, a scene of dramatic crisis, vibrating with
emotion and concentrated into four lines :

Anda, dímelo andando,
Dímelo andando,
Que si tú llevas miedo
Yo voy temblando.

Come, say it while walking,
Say it while walking,
For if you're full of fear
I am all trembling.

IV

The first circumstance that makes possible this striking condensation of dramatic interest is the strong structure of the copla. The three main types of coplas are the CUARTETA, the SOLEÁ and the SEGUIDILLA.[1]

The cuarteta is an octosyllabic quatrain, rhymed or, more frequently, assonanced, *abcb*. It may be metrically considered as the four first lines of a *romance*. It is solid and square like a stage, with its four corners clearly marked. It is undoubtedly the form most favourable for the dramatic song. The cuarteta is by far the most generally used form of copla and the only one which can be found in every part of Spain. The soleá or *solitude* (another name which is in itself a poem) is an octosyllabic tercet assonanced (or, more rarely, rhymed) *aba*.

> Me comparo con el cuervo.
> Todos visten de alegría :
> Yo visto de luto negro.

> I see myself as a crow.
> All are wearing clothes of gladness :
> Clothed in black mourning I go.

It is almost exclusively sung in the South. The Spanish ear is so used to the square rhythm of the cuarteta that the three-line rhythm produces an impression of unfulfilment rich in lyrical effect. There is a variety of soleá, the SOLEARIYA or *little solitude*, in which the first line is reduced to three syllables. The ALEGRÍA, or " mirth " is

---

[1] An excellent study of these and other forms of coplas will be found in an essay by D. Francisco Rodríguez Marín : 'La Copla, Bosquejo de un Estudio Folk-lórico.' Madrid, 1910.

also a beautiful lyrical copla, composed of only two
lines, the first of five (or six), the second of ten (or eleven)
syllables. It is also a Southern form. The only form
which can almost compete with the cuarteta in the range
of its sway is the seguidilla, a graceful copla composed of
two unrhymed heptasyllabics (first and third) and two
assonanced (or rhymed) pentasyllabics (second and fourth).

Del polvo de la tierra	Of the dust of the earth
Saco yo coplas.	Can I make songs.
No bien se acaba una	One is scarcely over,
Ya tengo otra.	A new one comes.

It moves with a dancing rhythm and lends itself particularly well to the light-hearted and to the satirical
veins, abundant in Spanish popular lyrics. The seguidilla
is sometimes, though not always, followed by a refrain or
ESTRIBILLO, which is another seguidilla, less its first line.

A la Cruz de la Encina	To the Cross of the Oak
No vayas, primo,	Don't go, my cousin,
Porque ya la paloma	For in her nest the dove
No està'n el nío.	You'll find no longer.
Primo, no vayas,	Cousin, don't go,
Porque ya, la paloma	For in her nest the dove
No està'nde estaba.	You'll find no more.

There is a variety of this copla, called SEGUIDILLA
GITANA (gypsy). The following beautiful example may
stand with advantage in lieu of a tedious description :

La ovejita es blanca,	The ewe lamb is white,
El praíto es verde,	And the meadow, green,
Y el pastorcito—madre,	And the little shepherd—oh
que la guarda	mother, who guards her
De peniya muere.	Is dying with grief.

This variety represents, as will be easily observed by the example quoted, the return of the rhythm of mirth and satire to the lyrical, plaintive tone which predominates in the South. For, despite their minute dimensions, the poetical forms of our popular lyrics are definite, complete and full of variety: instruments well built and tuned for all the moods of the popular muse.

A second and an even more important cause of the dramatic concentration of the copla is the admirable energy of the Castilian language, that " stateliest of the daughters of the Latin, not clipped and cut short like the hungry French, which devours so many of its syllables, not emasculated like the Italian, nor eviscerated like the Portuguese."[1] The Spanish people possess a deep instinct of the intrinsic value of words, and, contrary to what is the rule among the middle classes and even among certain half-" cultured " popular classes, such as workers in urban districts, they are sententious and measured in their speech. For words are symbols of spiritual or intellectual values just as money is a symbol of material wealth, and the more meaning we put into words the fewer words need we give away in token for the same weight of meaning. It is enough to hear and see a Spanish peasant speak such words as " un hombre," " un querer," " una madre," in order to realise that he speaks in earnest and with all the weight of a philosophy and all the impulse of a manly will behind his words. There is a story of an Andalucian " Capataz " (a foreman of farm labourers) who met his landowner in the early hours of the morning. It was in a season of severe drought and a little rain had fallen during the night. The landowner

[1] 'Calderón,' by Archbishop Trench. 2nd ed, 1886. P, 57.

asked : " Has it rained, Manuel ? "   And the capataz
answered : " As for raining, raining, it did rain. But
raining, RAINING, what you call RAINING, it has not
rained."

The tale is an excellent example of that dramatic
instinct for language, which feels the living and concrete
meaning of the word as different from the dead abstraction pinned in the dictionary like a dead butterfly in a
collection. And this capacity for filling up words with
an over-meaning of sense and intention, this special
power of symbolisation, is the faculty which best explains
the dramatic and lyrical intensity of the copla.

For the copla, though dramatic in its exposition, is
generally lyrical in its spirit and effect. When the scene
is over, an emotion lingers in the air and, far from
vanishing, becomes deeper and deeper as the mind
penetrates into the intimate significance, the lyrical
soul of the song. Listen to this simple song, which
evokes an innocent, an almost childish seascape, painted
on the shores of the Mediterranean :

Ay, no hay naíta que vê,	Lo, there is nothing to see,
Porque un barquiyo que había	For the little boat there was
Tendió la vela y se fué.	Spread its sails and went away.

The song will fly, and the sound of the voice will die
out. But you will be left musing, feeling the trail of
emotion left behind by the little boat that went away.
You will remember, not without regret, many a moment
of your life when things and people that " were there,"
" spread their sails and went away," and you were left
alone, and looked about you with dim eyes and thinking

that " there was nothing to see." For this copla, which
seems so simple and childish, is impregnated with the
essence of all departures and all farewells.

V

The capacity for concentrating in a few words the
quintessence of many moments and moods is an eminently poetical virtue ; it implies creative power, for to
create, in art, is to put spirit into the matter of the art,
in this case, words. But it supposes also that quality of
the soul which we call delicacy, a veil that covers the
bareness of our feelings, hides away their crudeness and
gives them charm and æsthetic value. The Spanish
people, even in their outbursts of most plebeian passion,
possess to an eminent degree this precious quality.
Witness the following typical coplas :

> Ay, madre, que me lo han roto,
> El cantarillo en la fuente.
> Yo no siento el cantarillo
> Sino qué dirá la gente.
>
> Ay de mí, que me han quitado
> Una rosa siendo mía.
> La veo en manos de otro,
> Marchita y descolorida.
>
> Viendo que no me querías
> A un arroyuelo bajé.
> Oí cantar a un jilguero.
> A escucharle me paré.
>
> Yo no digo que mi barca
> Sea la mejor del puerto.

Lo que sí digo es que tiene
Los mejores movimientos.

Oh, mother, they have broken
My pitcher at the fountain.
I do not mind the pitcher,
I mind what they will say.

Woe is me, for I am robbed
Of a rose that was my own.
I see it in other hands
Withered and its colour gone.

Seeing that you do not love me
I went towards a rivulet.
I heard a linnet singing there.
I stayed to hear it.

I do not say that my boat
Is the best in all the bay.
But that she is the most graceful
In her movements, I do say.

All these coplas are symbols of facts and situations
which remain veiled though not entirely concealed in
the song; and it should be noted that this facility for
expressing ideas by means of symbols, or parables, implies a rich poetical imagination not merely in the anonymous author who first sang the copla " out of his own
head," but also in his ever-growing audience and in
the people who adopt it and preserve it in the living
archives of their verbal tradition. There exists, then,
in the ranks of the Spanish people what amounts to a
spontaneous poetical culture which, self-ignorant though

it is, is nevertheless a great national asset, both as a creative and as a critical force.

This delicacy in the creation and the perception of poetical symbols does not exclude strength. Far from it, Spanish popular poetry often reveals a primitive vigour and an almost barbaric virginity in the emotions expressed. Its psychology is based on love, man-and-woman love, and, in a lower but perhaps intenser key, the love for the mother, an emotion deeply and gravely felt by the Spanish popular muse. Curiously enough, and perhaps unexpectedly for those who entertain but superficial or second-hand ideas about the Spanish people, the love copla is not particularly nor even predominantly sensuous. True, it can express desire with its usual pith and intensity :

Amantito, amantito,	Sweet lover, oh sweet lover,
Amante, amante,	When thee I sight,
Las pestañas me estorban	Even my own eyelashes
Para mirarte.	Are in my light.

Arrímate a mi querer,	Come close to my love
Como las salamanquesas	As lizards do to the wall.
Se arriman a la pared.	

Cuando paso por tu vera
Y me rosa tu vestío
Jasta los güesos me tiemblan.

When I pass close by your side
The very touch of your dress
Makes my bones shake in my body.

But even in these coplas intensity of feeling is attained

through a sobriety of expression which is in itself chaste, and which would be sufficient to reveal the existence of deep spiritual feelings, elevating and sanctifying carnal love. Deeply loving, the Spanish people are chaste of body and spirit. Their idea of love partakes of that almost religious austerity which is one of the typical features of the race, and sets it in a class apart not only in the so-called Latin, but in the European world. Thus numberless coplas of love turn on this idea that love is a thing of the soul :

> Aunque deje de mirarte,
> ¿ Qué importa ver o no ver ?
> Los gustos que son del alma
> Tambien un ciego los vé.

> ¿ Para qué vas preguntando
> Cómo se quiere de veras ?
> Si el querer está en el alma
> Y tú has nacido sin ella.

Though I may look at you no more,
What matters, see or not see ?
Pleasures that are of the soul
Even a blind man can see.

Why do you go about asking
How to love with a love true ?
Love is a thing of the soul,
A soul never was in you.

In this last copla the idea is expressed with great clearness. *Love is a thing of the soul*. This line is worthy of standing by the most famous cuarteta in perhaps the most famous play of Calderón, his admirable "Alcalde de Zalamea":

> Al Rey la hacienda y la vida
> Se ha de dar; pero el honor
> Es patrimonio del alma,
> Y el alma sólo es de Dios.

> To the King, our wealth and life
> We shall give, if give we must.
> But honour is the soul's patrimony,
> And the soul belongs to God.

The central idea of this manly assertion of the rights of the individual reappears as a frequent motive in many a copla of love:

> Me mandastes a decir
> Que era tuya el alma mía,
> Y yo te mandé a decir
> Que era de Dios, tuya y mía.

> El corazón te daré,
> También te daré la vida,
> Y el alma no te la doy
> Porque esa prenda no es mía.

> Te quiero mas que a mi vida
> Y mas que a mi corazón,
> Y mas que al alma no digo
> Porque se la debo a Dios.

> Thou sent'st me a message
> That my soul was thine.
> And I answered thee
> 'Twas God's, thine and mine.

I shall give you all my heart,
I shall give you all my life,
But my soul I shall not give you
For that treasure is not mine.

I love you more than my life,
I love you more than my heart.
I don't say more than my soul
For my soul I owe to God.

With this light in our mind we shall be able to pene-
trate into the exquisite obscurity of the following song,
which may be heard in the high valleys of the Asturian
Pyrenees :

Una niña bonita	A pretty maid
Se asomó a su balcón.	Leaned over her window.
Ella me pidió el alma,	She asked for my soul,
Yo la dí el corazón,	I gave her my heart,
Ella me pidió el alma,	She asked for my soul,
Y yo la dije adiós.	And I said farewell.

All these examples are, I hope, amply sufficient to
show that " love is a thing of the soul " for the Spanish
people. And that is why that curious word " querer,"
which our people always use instead of both " amar," to
love, and " amor," love, has in their speech and poetry
so much strength, or as they would say with another
admirable word, so much " virtud." But doubts might
be entertained as to the sincerity of a feeling precisely
because it is so clearly and definitely expressed. In
matters of feeling, an indirect and incidental suggestion
is often more convincing than a plain and simple statement. Spanish popular poetry abounds in such eloquent

sidelights, which leave no room for doubt as to the depth,
earnestness and spiritual character of love as understood
by the Spanish people :

> Quiéreme poco a poco
> No te apresures,
> Que lo que yo deseo
> Es que me dure.

> Tu querer y mi querer
> Son como el agua del río
> Que atrás no pueden volver.

> Tengo una cosa en mi pecho
> Que a nadie se la diré.
> Mortificaré mi cuerpo
> Por darle gusto al querer.

> El querer es cuesta arriba,
> El olvidar, cuesta abajo.
> Cuesta arriba he de subir
> Aunque me cueste trabajo.

Love me little by little,
Be not in haste
For I would have a love
That long may last.

They are, your love and my love,
Like the water of the river,
Backwards they never can flow.

I feel something in my breast
Which I shall never reveal.
I shall mortify my body
In order to please my love.

> Loving is up hill,
> Down hill is forgetting.
> Up hill I shall go,
> Though it be hard work.

These coplas, and many more, could not have been created but under the inspiration of an idea of love as far removed from the splendid, but somewhat bestial, sensuality of Asia as from the bloodless abstractions of medieval romance. But along with depth of feeling Spanish coplas reveal a surprising degree of subtlety and penetration. Songs can be found on nearly every possible situation of mind or soul, from the simplest to the most complex, from the primitive to the most refined, covering an almost Shakespearean range of character and psychology. Here is a miniature Romeo and Juliet:

> Como dos árboles somos
> Que la suerte nos separa,
> Con un camino por medio,
> Pero se juntan las ramas.

> Like two trees we are
> By fate separated.
> The road is between
> But the boughs are mated.

Here is a miniature Hamlet:

El puente voy a pasar,	The bridge I must cross over,
No sé si lo pasaré.	I wonder whether I'll cross it.
Palabrita tengo dada,	I have given my word,
No sé si la cumpliré.	I wonder whether I'll hold it.

The following are remarkable, but by no means exceptional, instances of complexity of thought and situation :

> No sé que pena es mas honda,
> Si la pena que se canta
> O la pena que se llora.

> Amante mío del alma,
> Donde ha habido siempre habrá.
> Tus ojos quieren mirarme,
> Déjalos con libertad.

> No siento en el mundo más
> Que tener tan mal sonido,
> Siendo de tan buen metal.

> I know not which is more deep,
> Whether the grief that we sing
> Or else the grief we weep.

> Lover, lover of my soul,
> Where there was, there'll always be.
> Your eyes want to look at mine,
> Let them look in liberty.

> This thought I cannot endure
> That my ring should be so bad
> When my metal is so pure.

As for subtlety, the Spanish copla can sustain the comparison with the poems of those modern masters who have, as it were, specialised in it. Maeterlinck is not more elusively symbolical than the anonymous author of the Asturian copla already quoted :

> Una niña bonita . . .

Poetical moods that seem created among tired, refined civilisations, can be found now and then in coplas such as the following :

Como se gasta una piedra	As the water of the stream
En agua de una corriente	Wears the stone day by day
Así se me está gastando	So by loving you so much
El corazón de quererte.	I wear my heart away.

Cuando quise, no quisiste.	You did not want, when I wanted.
Ahora que quieres, no quiero.	Now I don't want, when you do.
Gozarás del amor triste	You will enjoy a sad love
Como yo gozé primero.[1]	Just as I did before you.

Dante G. Rossetti might have envied the delicacy of touch in the treatment, and of inspiration in the theme, of this beautiful Asturian song, so poetically wrapped in the folds of its symbols :

> Tengo de subir, subir,
> Tengo de subir al puerto,
> Aunque me cubra la nieve.
> Si la nieve resbala,

[1] I have my doubts as to the popular origin of this copla. It is too well finished, rhymed throughout *abab*, instead of assonanced *abcb*, in the real popular fashion. Yet, I need not say that I fully endorse Señor Rodríguez Marín's criterion on this matter. A copla is as "popular" when *adopted* by the people as when created by them, and if and when the learned poet strikes the popular note to the point of succeeding in getting his copla adopted by the people, he must be considered as one of the people. Nor is it to be fancied that the people consider any *learned* song as worthy of the honour of popular adoption. The curious reader will find two interesting examples of "adoption" in Señor Rodríguez Marín's above-mentioned essay, in both of which the coplas written by middle-class poets underwent an anonymous transformation which greatly improved them both in common sense and in literary value.

¿ Qué hará la rosa ?
Ya se va marchitando
La mas hermosa.
¡ Ay mi amor !
Si la nieve resbala,
¿ Qué haré yo ?

Tengo de subir al puerto,
Aunque me cubra la nieve,
Allí está la que yo quiero.
Si la nieve resbala,
¿ Qué hará el sendero ?
Ya se va marchitando
La que yo quiero.
¡ Ay mi amor !
Si la nieve resbala,
¿ Qué haré yo ?

I must climb, must climb the hill,
I must climb up to the pass,
Though the snow may cover me.
If the snow should slide,
What will the rose do ?
The most beautiful one
Is beginning to wither.
Oh, my love !
If the snow should slide
What shall I do ?

I must climb up the pass
Though the snow may cover me,
For there is she whom I love.
If the snow should slide
What will the path do ?
She whom I love

> Is beginning to wither.
> Oh, my love !
> If the snow should slide
> What shall I do ?

It is impossible to imagine any poetry more exquisitely suggestive than this popular poetry grown wild among the snow of the Asturian mountains, so closely akin to, though wholly ignorant of, the art of Maeterlinck, Rossetti and the symbolist school. And it may even be of interest to remark that this curious variety of Spanish popular lyricism is particularly to be found in regions where earth and sky are grey, and the whole nature seems to brood with Northern lightlessness. In its most typical form, however, Spanish popular poetry is more primitive and more profound, more direct and more penetrating, and in its interpretation of nature and life, more virile than the refined yet somewhat effeminate poetry of modern symbolism. Its wealth of images is a byword and extends to all kinds of objects, alive or lifeless; astronomy:

> Las estrellitas del cielo
> Las cuento y no están cabales.
> Faltan la tuya y la mía
> Que son las más principales.

> I count the stars of heaven,
> Their number does not square.
> Your star and mine are missing
> And they are the most fair.

industry :

> Como los railitos del tren
> Son tu cariño y el mío,
> Porque van el uno juntito del otro,
> Tóo seguío, tóo seguío.

> Like the rails of a railway
> Are your love and my love,
> For they go together, each close to the other,
> All the way, all the way.

and even domestic utensils, for the Spanish popular muse is a busy housewife who sings while at work and is on excellent terms with things familiar and useful :

Tus ojos son dos tinteros,	Your eyes two ink-wells seem,
Tu nariz, pluma delgada.	Your nose, a pen well cut.
Tus dientes, letra menuda,	Your teeth are minute writing,
Tu pecho, carta cerrada.	Your breast, a letter shut.

Notice how this copla, which begins with a somewhat futile comparison, is redeemed by the grace of the image in the third line, and by the really poetical thought of the last.

VI

That facility for expressing itself in images which is readily recognised in Spanish poetry is not due to mere wanton and unguided imagination. Were they void of a real and positive value as symbols of those invisible links of natural sympathy which go from thing to thing under the surface of appearances, metaphors would be vain exercises of fancy and would lack that subtle power they have for setting us in a brooding mood. No one can find a just metaphor who is not possessed of a synthetic sense of reality ; that is why metaphors rarely visit men who are not poets—who seek them—or philosophers—who run shy of them, unless they cover their faces with ashes and call themselves *ideas*.

The wealth of metaphors and images which shines in the coplas is, therefore, a sure sign that the Spanish people feel nature as poets, in its entirety. For them " all is one and the same " : the stars, the earth, the sea, animals, society and man are different forms of one essence, which flows and transfigures itself under harmoi ious laws. Possessed of this transcendent feeling of unity, the deeper for being unconscious, the Spanish anonymous and collective poet naturally reaches that divine incoherence which is only attained by the greatest of the poets of culture—an apparent incoherence, but in truth the freedom of movement of those who feel themselves guided by the spirit of things. It is this supreme poetic gift which allows the poet to soar above the hedges of logic, and to look at nature with the width and loftiness of view which we like to fancy that birds enjoy. There is many a soaring copla in the ever-growing and living book of Spanish popular poetry :

Sarga la luna y alumbre	Let the moon rise and illumine
Er campo y los olivares.	The fields and the olive-groves.
Este querer que yo tengo	This love that rises in me
De los reaños me sale.	Springs from the depths of my body.

But there is another aspect of this incoherence which deserves to be noticed, namely the suggestion of the infinite complexity of things, only reducible to a unity in flashes of poetical vision. Hence that striking device of the independent refrain which usually follows the copla in most forms of Spanish popular music—"soleares," " alegrías," and even the universal and primitive JOTA. It is a copla in itself, wholly independent and irrelevant

in its substance from the main one, yet by its very irrele-
vance rich in artistic effect, even when it does not add
a deep philosophic sense to the mood of the main current
of song, as is the case with the following delightful
refrain, often heard in Andalucía :

> A mí se me da muy poco
> Que un pájaro en la alamea
> Se pasee de un arbo' a otro.

> It matters little to me
> That a bird among the poplars
> Should flutter from tree to tree.

One thinks of Shakespeare and his admirable use of
apparently irrelevant songs (Ophelia's songs, for instance)
as lyrical commentary to his drama ; but it is not only
in this that Shakespeare and the Spanish popular poets
can be compared ; it is also in their curious way of
bridging over the gulf between man and nature with
bold bridges of poetry :

> Blow, blow, thou winter wind,
> Thou art not so unkind
> As man's ingratitude. . . .

Fuentecilla cristalina.
Arroyuelo caudaloso,
Para dos que bien se quieren
Caminos largos son cortos.

Crystal-like spring,
Deep-flowing brook,
For loving couples
Long roads are short.

A los árboles altos
Los mueve el viento.
Y a los enamorados,
El pensamiento.

High trees are moved
By wanton winds.
Lovers are moved
By thoughts and dreams,

El querer que me tenías	The love you once had for me
En una fuente quedó.	By a spring you left one day.
Vino un fuerte remolino,	A strong gust of wind blew suddenly,
Rama y tronco se llevó.	Branch and stem it took away.
En el pozo mas hondo	In the deepest well
De mi corazón,	Of my heart I threw
Sembré una pasionera,	Seed of passion-flower,
Cogí una pasión.	And a passion grew.

But perhaps these examples will have brought to the reader's mind the poems of that great English genius whose poetry, more than any other, resembles in spirit and form the poetry of the Spanish people. In his pure and innocent individualism, in his courageous and lofty amorality, in his disinterestedness and utter lack of meanness, in that virility of his idea of love, so free and so chaste, and lastly in his almost mystic feeling of reality, William Blake is the poet whose spirit is in closest sympathy with the spirit of Spain and her people. He sang of innocence and experience, and his poetry is thus rich in songs and in proverbs. The same words apply literally to the poetry of the Spanish people, whose stock of love-songs is no less wonderful than their stock of proverbs, though less universally known through lack of a pedlar of genius, like Sancho, to spread them over the earth. Blake's world is the same as that of the Spanish coplas, midway between the human soul and nature :

> A flower was offered me,
>   Such a flower as May never bore.
> But I said : " I've a pretty rose-tree,"
>   And I passed the sweet flower o'er.

> Then I went to my pretty rose-tree,
>   To tend her by day and by night ;
> But my rose turned away with jealousy
> And her thorns were my only delight.

This is exactly the tone of the Spanish copla, and this is its symbolism which sees in natural objects the most complex states of mind, and speaks of trees and flowers as if they were human beings :

Arbolito, te secaste,	Little tree, you withered,
Teniendo la fuente al pie,	Having the spring at your feet,
En el tronco la firmeza,	Fortitude, in your stem, having,
Y en la ramita, el querer.	And in your little branch, love.

That Blakeian exquisite delicacy in the choice of symbols which veil, yet reveal, the mysteries of thought, can be admired in Spanish coplas as well as in Blake's poems. Thus it is easy to find three coplas to match each of the three delightful stanzas of the following poem:

> Never seek to tell thy love,
>   Love that never told can be ;
> For the gentle wind doth move
>   Silently, invisibly.

> I told my love, I told my love,
>   I told her all my heart,
> Trembling, cold, in ghastly fears,
>   Ah ! she did depart !

> Soon after she was gone from me,
>   A traveller came by,
> Silently, invisibly :
>   He took her with a sigh.

The thought expressed in the first stanza appears in this copla :

Que te quiero, bien lo sabes,	That I love you, you know well.
Pero no lo comunico	But nor you nor anybody
Ni contigo ni con nadie.	I shall ever tell.

The admirable dramatic concentration of the second stanza can be compared with that of a copla which has already been quoted :

Anda, dímelo andando,	Come, say it while walking,
Dímelo andando.	Say it while walking.
Que si tú llevas miedo	For if you're full of fear
Yo voy temblando.	I am all trembling.

And as for the ending, so deeply felt and so lightly expressed, here is a copla which need not fear a comparison either in simplicity or in the ingenuous art of its composition, and is perhaps richer than Blake's own stanza in freshness, colour and exquisite scent :

Ar pie del armendro estuve	I was at the foot of the almond-tree
Y no le cogí la flô.	And did not take its blossom.
Asín que m'arretiré	As soon as I went away
Otro llegó y la cogió.	A stranger came and took it.

The following lines might be thought to be by Blake :

> Rose, if I did not take thee
> 'Twas because I did not choose.
> I slept under the rose-tree.
> I had for my bed a rose.

They are a literal translation of a Spanish popular song :

> Rosa, si no te cogí
> Fué porque no tuve gana.
> Al pie del rosal dormí.
> La rosa tuve por cama.

There is a tenderness worthy of Blake's " Songs of Innocence " in this song :

Manzanita colorada	Ruddy little apple
Que en el suelo te cogí,	Whom I picked up,
Si no estás enamorada,	If thou art not in love
Enamórate de mi.	Fall in love with me.

There is a wealth and an extravagance of imagination worthy of the Blake of the " Auguries of Innocence " in the gipsy curse set in this other copla :

Tóitas las arañas negras	May all the black spiders
Que están metía 'n sus nidos	Hidden in their nests
Me pique 'n er corasón	Sting me in the heart
Si mi querer es fingío.	If my love is feigned.

And there is a philosophy of love worthy of the poet who wrote " The Clod and the Pebble " in this little poem of melancholy wisdom :

> Tu querer es como el pozo
> Que cuesta sacarle el agua.
> Y el mío es como la fuente,
> Que ella sola se derrama.

> Your love is a well, whose water
> Must be with effort drawn up.
> And mine is a spring, whose water
> Of itself comes out.

VII

Further quotation is unnecessary in order to establish the close relationship between Blake's poetry and the poetry of the Spanish people, and therefore the depth and originality of the philosophy which inspires the copla. It is a philosophy wise in its acceptance of things as they are, penetrating in its interpretation of the facts of nature and their intimate connections ; which turns to nature in search of the eternal answers to the eternal questions and clasps with a brooch of poetry the cycle that goes from man to things and from things to man :

> Del rosal sale la rosa.
> De la maceta, el clavel.
> Un padre cría a una hija
> Y no sabe para quíén.

> From the rose bush comes the rose.
> From the flow'r-pot, the pink-bloom.
> A father brings up a daughter
> And he does not know for whom.

It is a philosophy that feels life in all its forms with that human intensity which vibrates in the tortured lines of Blake.

> Cuando una mata se muere
> Al tronco llega el dolor.
> Las raíces lloran sangre,
> De luto viste la flor.

> When a plant dies
> The pain reaches the stem,
> The roots weep tears of blood,
> The flower puts on mourning.

It is a philosophy which, like that of Blake, is indifferent, with the detachment of contemplative souls, to the changes of worldly fortune—unstable, futile, and devoid of all permanent sense. This indifference is often expressed in coplas as light and airy as fortune itself ; witness that refrain already quoted :

> It matters little to me
> That a bird among the poplars
> Should flutter from tree to tree . . .

A sublime indifference towards worldly things which borders on fatalism. There is no lack of fatalistic coplas, some almost Asiatic in their passivity :

> Las estrellas corren, corren . . .
> Yo no tengo de correr.
> Donde me pilla la noche
> Allí tengo 'amanecer.

> The stars run and run,
> I need not run as they do.
> Where night overtakes me
> There I will see the dawn.

Others in which fatalism inspires faith and courage when the aim is high enough, and no aim is higher than true love :

> Cuando se quiere de veras
> No se mira al qué dirán.
> Quién tiene fé en el camino
> No vuelve la vista atrás.

> The true lover is not daunted
> By his neighbour's idle talk.
> He who has faith in his road
> Backwards never casts his eyes.

Yet fatalism is, perhaps, less essential an element of our people's character than it is generally supposed. True, it is there, and can be felt in the curious attitude of the Spaniard towards life, acutely seen, accepted, but neither approved nor disapproved, neither enjoyed nor suffered. But in this attitude, fatalism is more like a hue or a fleeting scent than like a constituent element. Let him who would doubt it bear in mind how frequently appears in Spanish literature, in the classics no less than in popular songs, the theme of " Hombría," manliness, the over-powering " Yo," imposing his will over things, men, and even destiny :

> Lo que intento, logro.
> Yo no me quejo 'e mi estrella.
> Que yo no he intentado cosa
> Que no me salga con ella.

> What I try, I conquer.
> Of my star I don't complain.
> I never aimed at a thing
> Which I did not gain.

A restrained but forceful assertion of victory. Here is, in contrast, the stoic acceptance of defeat, not less manly in its refusal of pity :

> Náide me tenga doló,
> Que yo por mis propias manos
> M'he buscao mi perdisión

> Let no one pity me,
> I, myself, with my own hands
> Was the cause of my undoing.

And with stoicism it is well to close this sketch of Spanish character as revealed by the songs of the Spanish people. The senses look outward and see reality in the world. The heart looks inwards and sees reality in the soul. World and the soul are linked by poetry in a fraternity of exile. But the manly spirit rises up against adversity and fate, accepts life as it is, does not complain, does not ask for pity. Thus went the thoughts of Seneca, the Spanish Roman. Thus still run the thoughts of the Spanish people, the people-poet, which knows how to make of song its deepest philosophy :

> El que quiera cantar bien
> Cante cuando tenga pena,
> Que la misma pena le hace
> Cantar bien aunque no sepa.

He who would care to sing well
Let him sing when grieved at heart,
Though he know nothing of singing
Grief will take the place of art.

THE CASE OF WORDSWORTH

THE CASE OF WORDSWORTH

In the preface to his edition of Wordsworth's poems (1879), Matthew Arnold made three observations which still hold good to-day, viz. :

1. That Wordsworth was not recognised abroad as what, in Matthew Arnold's opinion, he was, the greatest English poet since Shakespeare and Milton and the greatest in Europe after Molière and Goethe.

2. That there were Wordsworthians. This, I may add, is a curious fact, and worthy of attention, though Matthew Arnold refers to it incidentally and as a matter of course. Why should there be Wordsworthians and not Shakespeareans, Miltonians or Shelleyans? And moreover, why should Wordsworthians be so sensitive?

3. That Wordsworthians, even when ready to admit that the poet dozed now and then, read everything he wrote :

"But I am a Wordsworthian myself. I can read with pleasure and edification *Peter Bell*, and the whole series of *Ecclesiastical Sonnets*, and the address to Mr. Wilkinson's Spade, and even the *Thanksgiving Ode* ;—everything of Wordsworth, I think, except *Vandracour and Julia*."

Any attempt at interpreting Wordsworth must provide a plausible explanation of these three persistent facts.

"If," wrote Matthew Arnold, "Wordsworth's place among the poets who have appeared in the last two or three centuries is after Shakespeare, Molière, Milton, Goethe, indeed, but before all the rest, then in time Wordsworth will have his due. We shall recognise him

in his place, as we recognise Shakespeare and Milton; and
not only we ourselves shall recognise him, but he will be
recognised by Europe also."

Up to the present day, however, this prophecy has not
come true. Nor is it possible to argue, with Matthew
Arnold, that Europe was slow also in recognising Shakespeare and Milton, for present-day Europe has achieved
a unity of culture unknown in Matthew Arnold's time,
let alone in that of the " Biographie Universelle," which
he quotes as an example of foreign inability to understand Shakespeare. Nowadays the relatively small community of men of letters who study and speak for Europe
cannot be said to be hindered by any provincialism of
taste in their estimate of an English poet. English is
one of the three or four great languages of the world.
It is not the veil of ignorance which stands between the
world and Wordsworth's glory. If then Europe has not
yet " recognised " Wordsworth, it is perhaps not too
rash to assume that she never will. We are then con-
fronted with a question of fact. In England, a considerable body of literary opinion, following Matthew
Arnold, holds Wordsworth a glorious third after Shakespeare and Milton. In Europe, Wordsworth is hardly
known to the reading many and is not considered as a
universal poet by the discerning few. A consistent interpretation of his work and character may perhaps provide an explanation of this discrepancy as well as of the
two other facts observed by Matthew Arnold and which
form with it *the Case of Wordsworth*.

Universal fame goes to the powerful. Power is the
magnet which draws admiration towards such dissimilar

figures as Æschylus, Hernán Cortés and Newton. But power may reside in the will, and govern men and things, and then its road to glory is through action ; or it may reside in the spirit, and then its road to glory is one of the three avenues which lead to the Absolute—the True, the Good, the Beautiful.

It is too readily assumed that the True, the Good and the Beautiful are one and the same thing. They are. We want them to be. We passionately want them to be, and that is why we keep proving it through ages of philosophy. But even *if* they are, even *though* they are, one and the same thing, it is only in the Infinite, parallel ideas that meet in the lap of God as verticals meet in the centre of the earth. And, even as geometrically parallel lines, they never meet for practical purposes.

It is the mark of our limitation that we cannot achieve within ourselves the ideal synthesis of the three essences of the spirit, and that all our attempts are doomed to result in confusion, error and ugliness. Yet the three essences are present in all of us, though in varying degrees, and in most of us one of them predominates, to the prejudice, be it noted, not to the advantage, of the other two. Thus our character will be influenced by a predominant sense of beauty, or of truth, or of virtue, and, whatever philosophy may say, instinct and experience show that each of these three types possesses pronounced features not merely different from, but even in opposition to, those of the other two. With some exceptionally gifted children of nature the influence of one of the three essences of the spirit is so strong that their being is overbalanced. They are the predestined, the Princes of the Spirit, Poets, Philosophers, Saints.

WORDSWORTH AND BEAUTY

> Oh ! many are the poets that are sown
> By nature ; men endowed with highest gifts,
> The vision and the faculty divine,
> Yet wanting the accomplishment of verse.
>
> WILLIAM WORDSWORTH.

A POET is a worshipper of Beauty. There is no true worship without faith. A poet is therefore a man who has put his faith in Beauty. Beauty is the star that guides his steps and he needs no other light. Other things equal, the purer his devotion to Beauty, the greater the poet. It is only by strict fidelity to one of the three stars of the spirit that genius can achieve entire freedom over time and space, incident and circumstance, and make his kingdom as wide as the world and as lasting as life. Just as our eyes transform into light all sensations, so a poet transforms into beauty all experience. He is in the midst of nature like a sonorous echo,

> Mon âme aux mille voix que le Dieu que j'adore
> Mit au centre de tout comme un écho sonore,

an echo open to all voices, vibrating to all sounds. He is content to sing, and he leaves to nature the task of harmonising his songs with the movements of the stars and the actions of men.

This does not mean that the poet is not to have a synthetic intuition of the world. Such an intuition is, on the contrary, the very ground in which the poetic

faculty takes root. It may indeed be noticed that in
current speech the word Poet often means little else than
a person possessing that vision which can embrace the
world as a whole. Wordsworth used the word in that
sense when he said :

> Oh ! many are the poets that are sown
> By nature ; men endowed with highest gifts,
> The vision and the faculty divine,
> Yet wanting the accomplishment of verse.[1]

And provided the last line is properly interpreted, this
passage is a not inadequate description of Wordsworth
himself.

In this first and somewhat vague sense, Wordsworth
is indeed one of the great poets of the world. His mind
and soul, even his senses, seem to be steeped in the feeling
of the unity of things. He means nothing else when he
says :

> To every natural form, rock, fruits, or flower,
> Even the loose stones that cover the highway,
> I gave a moral life ;

which is merely another formula for what he expresses
much better two lines below :

> and all
> That I beheld respired with inward meaning.[2]

It is in this that he was greatest. He was endowed with
" the vision and the faculty divine " of seeing the inward
relations between natural things, whether human, animal
or inanimate, and therefore, of looking at the meanest
flower that blows with an eye and a mind that had in
them the image of the whole world. His thought was

[1] " Excursion."   [2] " Prelude." 3rd book,

high and vast. He is a star of the first magnitude in the English literary firmament. For the greatness of a writer must be measured by the breadth and spaciousness of his sphere of work. The two master qualities of literary greatness are imagination and power. Imagination is the light that enlarges our world. Power sustains our wings and allows us to carry achievement as far as vision has carried desire. Power and imagination are as it were the body and the soul of greatness. Wordsworth was rich in both, and his work is a great work. It has spaciousness. It has elevation. Here and there it has depth. And it is full of life, not merely of the amorphous substance of life, but of the infinite number of creatures, stars and flowers and stones, mountains and valleys, seas and rivers and a multitude of human beings. It is indeed a work so spacious and peopled that one might think it a world, like that of Shakespeare or Lope de Vega. Yet, it is not a world, but a picture. And why? Because all these creatures are looking the same way, like cattle at sunset.

It is here, in my opinion, that Wordsworth's claim to count as a great poet fails. For a great poet in the real and complete sense of the word is not merely a writer endowed with the vision and the faculty divine, but a creator capable of growing from this soil of intuition flowers of art, creations living a life of their own and therefore reflecting in their variety the divine variety of nature. That Wordsworth might have been such a creator there is not the slightest doubt. The man who could write the " Lucy " sequence and sonnets like

" Mutability " or " Surprised by Joy . . ." was born to
be a poet. Yet, he failed to live up to his gifts, and left
but a few genuine poems lost in an imposing work of an
essentially unpoetical character.

The usual accusation against Wordsworth is that he
endeavoured to write poetry on " trivial " or " low "
incidents, and, despite his own and many more brilliant
defences of his doctrine and practice, this opinion still
survives. It is of course untenable. The sun will turn
into a diamond the humblest pebble on the road. Poetry
will turn to beauty the " lowest " and most " trivial "
fact. Neither this dispute on the subject, nor the
" poetic diction " dispute on the language, of poetry, are,
I venture to think, in the least helpful towards the eluci-
dation of the case of Wordsworth. Language and subject are after all but accidents in poetry. The essence of
poetry is the *mood*, and it is only by an examination of
the mood in which Wordsworth wrote that we can hope
to arrive at an understanding of his work.

It must, however, be pointed out that Wordsworth's
opinions on the subjects fit for poetry were not so far
from those of his opponents as might be thought. When
attacked by parodists and such-like literary insects on
account of his simplicity of diction, he quoted Dr.
Johnson's stanza :

> I put my hat upon my head
> And walked into the Strand,
> And there I met another man
> Whose hat was in his hand.

And, comparing it with a stanza from " The Babes in the
Wood," which he gives as " admirable," he concludes :

" Whence arises this difference ?   Not from the metre, not from the language, not from the order of the words ; but the *matter* expressed in Dr. Johnson's stanza is contemptible."[1]

Now, there is a Spanish popular song, quite a little poem, which differs very little in its *matter* from Dr. Johnson's lines :

> Por la calle abajito
> Va quien yo quiero.
> No le veo la cara
> Por el sombrero.[2]

Whence arises this difference ? may we ask again. Merely from the mood. Dr. Johnson wrote his quatrain in the mood of a very poor parodist. The unknown girl who first sang the little song was in love and saw her lover pass in the street, and tried this way and that to see his face and gave it up because his hat was in her light. It may be argued that there is here a considerable difference in *matter*, but it is only inasmuch as it is a difference in mood that it affects the poetical value of the poems compared.

I have quoted this Spanish song as an example because Spanish popular poetry succeeds—without attempting— in achieving what Wordsworth attempted without success. Spanish popular poetry answers all the requirements of Wordsworth's theory.   It is cast in the simplest

---

[1] Preface to the second edition of 'Lyrical Ballads' (1800). *Cf.* several lines above in the same Preface : ". . . I may have written upon unworthy subjects."

[2] Literally :   Down the street goes my lover ;
I cannot see his face under his hat.

possible diction, being expressed for, by and in the language of the people ; it dwells on everyday events and describes everyday scenes in simple and even homely images ; and, beyond the usual religious beliefs which can hardly be called supernatural, it never appeals to the weird, the fantastic, the unknown or the fabulous. Yet, though coincident in theory, it contrasts in practice with Wordsworth's own work, and particularly with his Lyrical Ballads, in its sobriety, its severe yet effective concision of detail, its absence of *pleading*, its extreme variety of tone and feeling and that exquisite sensation of completeness, both of form and substance, which it produces, and which is only comparable to the harmony of a perfect musical chord.

Here again the difference is one of mood. There is a certain similarity of attitude between Wordsworth and the Spanish anonymous popular poets : a quiet, long gaze at nature seems to be the starting-point in either case. But the Englishman loses in poetical inspiration by all the wealth of his ever-active and purposeful intellect. Humble and simple, the Spaniards leave their intellect at rest, or, better, limit its activities to the menial function which it must always fulfil in the house of the poet, while they look and listen to the ebb and flow between nature and their soul. The Englishman, *roseau pensant*, cannot prevent his thought from deflecting the flow into pregrooved channels. The flow, thus deflected, cools down, and inspiration dies.

It was Matthew Arnold who said that " in Wordsworth's case, the accident, for so it may almost be called, of inspiration, is of peculiar importance." The fact is that the mood in which Wordsworth wrote made inspira-

tion a very unlikely accident indeed. No poet ever wrote
under so close a watch of his conscious self. His intellect
never loosened its grip over his creative soul. All through
his work we can see the cold glare of his eye contemplating
the agitation below as the eye of a general his regiments
in battle. A word of explanation is perhaps needed here
since Wordsworth has usually been represented precisely
as the champion of instinct against intellect in poetry.
The origin of this, to my mind, mistaken opinion is that,
mainly as a reaction against his own Godwinian adventure, Wordsworth in his prose and verse often preached
the superiority of intuition and natural promptings over
mere reason. But when studying a poet we are not
concerned with his views so much as with his works. It
is not his theory but his practice that matters. One of
Wordsworth's most brilliant commentators gives the
following poem as an illustration of his anti-intellec-
tualism :

> Books ! 'tis a dull and endless strife :
> Come, hear the woodland linnet,
> How sweet his music ! on my life,
> There's more of wisdom in it.

> And hark ! how blithe the throstle sings !
> He, too, is no mean preacher :
> Come forth into the light of things,
> Let nature be your teacher.

> She has a world of ready wealtn,
> Our minds and hearts to bless—
> Spontaneous wisdom breathed by health,
> Truth breathed by cheerfulness.

One impulse from a vernal wood
May teach you more of man,
Of moral evil and of good,
Than all the sages can.

Sweet is the lore which nature brings ;
Our meddling intellect
Mis-shapes the beauteous forms of things :—
We murder to dissect.

This poem, excellent as a profession of Wordsworth's
anti-intellectual faith, is still better as an illustration of
his intellectualist practice. It is written in the brain. It
is full of teaching and preaching. It is not nature, but
nature through the " meddling " intellect. So were in
a greater or lesser degree, but always predominantly, all
but a handful of the poems which Wordsworth wrote.
That is why, rather than a great poet, he is an impressive
quarry of poetical ore which remains hard and cold for
lack of the fire of inspiration.[1]

[1] There is a page in Wordsworth's ' Observations to the Second Edition
of the Lyrical Ballads' which is truly illuminating as to his ideas on
poetry. It is his famous definition of the poet :—
"He is a man speaking to men ; a man, it is true, endued with more
lively sensibility, more enthusiasm and tenderness, who has a greater knowledge of human nature, and a more comprehensive soul, than are supposed to
be common among mankind ; a man pleased with his own passions and
volitions, and who rejoices more than other men in the spirit of life
that is in him ; delighting to contemplate similar volitions and passions as
manifested in the goings-on of the universe, and habitually impelled to
create them where he does not find them. To these qualities he has added
a disposition to be affected more than other men by absent things as if
they were present ; an ability of conjuring up in himself passions, which
are indeed far from being the same as those produced by real events, yet
(especially in those parts of the general sympathy which are pleasing and
delightful) do more nearly resemble the passions produced by real events
than any thing which, from the motions of their own minds merely, other

An important consequence is that Wordsworth's poetry usually lacks that unity of form which only inspiration can give. His poems are not born one, but put together. His form, therefore, is " patchy," firm and set modellings emerging here and there from a shapeless mass, as if the matter had been cast in broken or incomplete moulds. Thus, in one of his best poems he can write such lines as :

> This child I to myself will take

and, after a line of deplorable and inharmonious padding, set one of his finest gems :

> Nor shall she fail to see
> Even in the motions of the storm
> Grace that shall mould the maiden's form
> By silent sympathy.

His craftsmanship has been condemned even by Wordsworthians. But he can be a good craftsman when inspired. There is something here worse than a failure

men are accustomed to feel in themselves : whence, and from practice, he has acquired a greater readiness and power in expressing what he thinks and feels, and especially those thoughts and feelings which, by his own choice, or from the structure of his own mind, arise in him without immediate external excitement."

There is not too much "power in expressing what he thinks and feels" in this remarkable passage, which is perhaps a better definition of Wordsworth than of "the Poet." And not the least remarkable feature of it is the complete absence of the one element without which "the Poet" is not a poet, namely, inspiration. Another similar page occurs in the Preface to the Poems, published by Wordsworth in 1815. In this Preface the author enumerates "the powers requisite for the production of poetry," which in his view are : Observation and Description ; Sensibility ; Reflection ; Imagination and Fancy ; Invention and Judgment. "Sensibility to the harmony of numbers" and "the power of producing it" are relegated to a footnote as "invariably attendants upon the faculties above specified." Inspiration is not mentioned, not even incidentally.

in craftsmanship. The poet, after all, gives form to his works in no other wise than does the blacksmith. He hammers on and, when a shape is faulty, he softens the matter at the fire of his inspiration and hammers on again. Craftsmanship is of no avail if the fire of inspiration is out.[1]

It seldom burns for long in Wordsworth. The sense of exhilaration which it creates—not merely in the spirit, but in the very body of the poet—manifests itself in rhythm. Wordsworth is the poorest in rhythm of all great English poets. Indeed, that is not saying enough, for English poetry is exceptionally rich in rhythm. It is doubtful whether Wordsworth had even a clear idea of what rhythm is. Whenever he theorises on poetry, he refers only to rhyme and metre. Now, metre is to rhythm what the seven notes of the piano are to music, or the five lines of the score to the notes printed on them. Wordsworth does not seem to have understood the difference between the " score " of metrical arrangements, conventional though based on natural laws, and the spontaneous song of rhythm playing on it. This is a hard saying and one which cannot be advanced without diffidence. Yet, it is not easy to interpret otherwise the lack of rhythm, or worse still, of correspondence between rhythm and matter, in his writings, and the direct evi-

---

[1] Readers of Dorothy Wordsworth's Journals are familiar with the frequent compassionate notes of the devoted sister on " poor William " who has "tired himself out with composition." He evidently applied all his strength of will, which was great and unremitting, to the terrible task of hammering cold iron into shape. We owe to Miss Wordsworth a delightfully naïve little revelation which sheds much light on Wordsworth's habits of composition :—

"William tired himself with seeking an epithet for the cuckoo" (Friday, 14th May, 1802).

dence on the subject which he left in his prose works. It will be remembered that in his famous criticism of Gray's sonnet,[1] referring to the lines :

> I fruitless mourn to him that cannot hear
> And weep the more because I weep in vain,

he says :

"It will easily be perceived that the only part of this sonnet which is of any value is the lines printed in italics; it is equally obvious that, except in the rhyme, and in the use of the single word 'fruitless' for fruitlessly, which is so far a defect, the language of these lines does in no respect differ from that of prose."

This example goes far to show that Wordsworth was deaf to rhythm and saw nothing in poetry but metre and rhyme, and that "harmony in numbers" which derives from the mere flow of language between the banks of metre. But, if there were any doubt as to what he meant by this word *metre*, so often under his pen, metre, as he says, "regulated by strict laws," he has left numerous passages, any one of which should suffice to prove that he did not realise the existence in poetry of a spontaneous and substantial element of music above the adventitious and instrumental element of metrical arrangements. Thus, he has an ingenious theory of the soothing effect of the "continual and regular impulses of pleasurable surprise from the metrical arrangement" which he gives as proof of the utility of metre to make more bearable "the most pathetic scenes" of Shakespeare. He thinks of metre as of a merely adventitious element which the writer can if he so desires "superadd" (the very word is a final argument). He says as much in as clear a language

---

[1] "Observations to the Second Edition of the Lyrical Ballads."

as we can desire. " Metre is but adventitious to composition." Or, "Now, supposing for a moment that whatever is interesting in these objects may be as vividly described in prose, why am I to be condemned if to such description I have endeavoured to superadd the charm which by the consent of all nations is acknowledged to exist in metrical language?" And again: " To this language [that of the earliest poets] it is probable that metre of some sort or other was early superadded."

He thought apparently that the word *singing* applied to poets was a metaphor and does not seem to have suspected its accurate and literal meaning as truly and as soberly descriptive of poetry as of music.[1] He has been

[1] Wordsworth treats this subject in his 1815 Preface. His statements as to the relations between music and poetry are : (*a*) That "Epic Poets, in order that their mode of composition may accord with the elevation of their subject, represent themselves as *singing* from the inspiration of the Muse . . . but this is a fiction, in modern times, of slight value : the 'Iliad' or the 'Paradise Lost' would gain little in our estimation by being chanted. The other poets who belong to this class [the Narrative] are commonly content to tell their tale; so that of the whole it may be affirmed that they neither require nor reject the accompaniment of music." (*b*) " The Lyrical [form of poetry], containing the Hymn, the Ode, the Elegy, the Song and the Ballad ; in all of which, for the production of their *full* effect, an accompaniment of music is indispensable." (*c*) That "Poems, however humble in their kind, if they be good in that kind, cannot read themselves; the law of long syllable and short must not be so inflexible— the letter of metre must not be so impassive to the spirit of versification—as to deprive the reader of all voluntary power to modulate, in subordination to the sense, the music of the poem. . . . But, though the accompaniment of a musical instrument be frequently dispensed with, the true Poet does not therefore abandon his privilege distinct from that of the mere Proseman—

> ' He murmurs near the running brooks
> A music sweeter than their own.' "

It is only in (*c*) that Wordsworth seems to come near to the understanding of the rhythm that dances on the stage of metre, but he obviously clings to his idea that music is an afterthought in poetical creation instead of the very substance of it.

compared with Milton, and undoubtedly Wordsworth's voice has a sound not unlike that of Milton's voice. Dorothy Wordsworth has left us as good an explanation of this as we could wish. " William wrote two sonnets on Buonaparte, after I had read Milton's sonnets to him."[1] Wordsworth, however, speaks (when he does not talk), admonishes, advises, warns, tells, muses, but he never *sings :* while no poet, even in England, was better described than the immortal master of " Paradise Lost," " Lycidas," and the Sonnets, in the words of Verlaine's " Art Poétique."

> De la musique avant toute chose.

With him we are far from that poor, mechanical conception of *metre* which Wordsworth never surpassed in theory and seldom in practice. We have to go to the masters of music, to Bach himself, in order to find a fit comparison to that perfect opening of his great elegy :

> Yet once more, O ye laurels, and once more
> Ye myrtles brown. . . .

It cannot be counted against Wordsworth that he never sang in such great yet exquisite tones, but the reproach is legitimate that he lived all his life face to face with nature without ever trying to *sing* it. He describes or relates by a series of external touches of detail which grip the mind at too many points to let it vibrate ; for the mind is like a crystal bowl that rings only when lightly touched. He has written songs, that is, words for tunes already existing. He could also write good echoes of Milton, to

---

[1] Friday, May 21st, 1802. *Cf.* "I have been . . . repeating some of his sonnets to him, listening to his own repeating, reading some of Milton's and the 'Allegro' and 'Penseroso.'" D. W. J., December 24th, 1802.

whose voice he often listened with his usual application
and industry and with a lofty spirit not unlike the master's
own. The elevation of his thought and the sustained
power of his delivery achieve in his longer works a
" harmony in numbers " truly eloquent. But his only
original and personal rhythm is that of the *walker*.
Matthew Arnold gives as an example of his " characteristic form of expression " the following line from
" Michael " :

> And never lifted up a single stone.

This line is characteristic not merely for its somewhat
bare though noble simplicity, but also for its rhythm.
It is the walking pace, the pace of the Wanderer. There
is in Wordsworth too much composure, too much respectability, he is too much like a British gentleman in his
Sunday clothes to admit of any other gait than the
sober, steady, sure-footed walking. It is the dominant
rhythm of his mind, that mind of his which will not
spare the reader one single step in reasoning, description
or narrative. It regulates the progress of all his verse,
and it is never more triumphant than in the rare cases
when he tries to venture into more agitated or fanciful
movements. A case in point is his " Skylark." He
begins on a forced note, false and too buoyant :

> Up with me ! up with me into the clouds !

It is the false elation of an elderly clergyman trying to
be playful with the schoolboys. We hear him falling
heavily on the grass in the second line :

> For thy song, lark, is strong.

Yet he tries again, and for thirteen lines does his best to shout himself into the clouds with no better success ; then, his buoyancy exhausted, he falls back into the talking mood and resigns himself to walking again :

> I, with my fate contented, will plod on.

The contrast with a really poetical treatment of the same subject may be measured by merely comparing Wordsworth's first line with the first line of Shelley's " Skylark."

> Up with me ! up with me into the clouds !

fails to express what it says. Shelley, without saying anything about it, succeeds in expressing that skyward yearning which the contemplation of the skylark awakes in the poet's soul. He says anything, no matter what, but in words so thin, unearthly, weightless, that they instantly fly to heaven like an arrow of light :

> Hail to thee, blithe spirit !

How natural and spontaneous, yet how much more effective than Wordsworth's forced and willed lyricism ! To my mind, a similar objection, namely, that it is written in a mood of forced and self-conscious exaltation, may be raised against the famous ode. It is, properly speaking, a dissertation on immortality based on recollections of early childhood, to which metre has been " superadded." When we turn from the first line of any other great English ode,

> Thou still unravish'd bride of quietness . . .
> O wild West Wind, thou breath of Autumn's being . . .
> Season of mists and mellow fruitfulness . , ,

when we turn from these first lines which might just as
well be called " first bars " of great English odes, to the
first line of Wordsworth's own ode :

There was a time when meadow, grove, and stream . . .

we are struck by the difference between the song and the
tale. This beginning is but a statement of fact, clothed
though it is in rhetorical array. As we proceed, our impression grows that the poet is outside his poem. He is
not at the same time the subject and the object of his
song. He is not *sung through*, *played by*, the muses. He
is using his poem for a purpose. His images are in
reality but illustrations of a theory. He has something
to explain. How could he sing ? True, he says :

> My heart is at your festival,
> My head hath its coronal,
> The fullness of your bliss I feel, I feel it all,

but he wears his coronal at home, and it is through the
window of his study that he sees

> the young lamb's bound
> As to the tabor's sound,

and it is at his desk that he writes that cold, flat line :

> In years that bring the philosophic mind,

the most abrupt fall that ever broke the back of an ode.
An ode is a poem, and a poem is a flow of feeling with an
undercurrent of thought, while in this rhymed essay
thoughts and moods are not blended, but the line of
thought, settled beforehand, determines the sequence of
the moods in order to suit the argument. This excess
of intellectual control was to a considerable extent the

cause of the poverty and rigidity of Wordsworth's rhythm.

Hence, in spite of his marvellous gifts, his failure as a poet of nature. He was a good observer and knew and loved nature as it has never been known or loved before or since. He was therefore able to reproduce this or that movement, this or that murmur, this or that sound,[1] but he could not *symphonise* his impressions and merge them into the harmony of one eternal instant. He could not express a moment of nature with that admirable fidelity of emotional interpretation, that perfect fitness of tune and tone, music and mood, which Collins achieved once in his Ode to Evening. He never attained the unsought-for art of rendering the moods of nature by rhythms of the poet's own singing. This power which allows poetry to interpret nature with the most exquisite, yet spontaneous accuracy, is a free gift of the muses. The poet finds it in his song without having striven for it. It is the reward of his unreserved devotion to Beauty, of his absolute self-surrender to inspiration. When Wordsworth writes :

> Sweetest melodies
> Are those that are by distance made more sweet

he is *speaking*, though in "metre," and conveying to the reader a piece of information. (In actual fact, as will be seen by a perusal of the poem, "Personal Talk," he is *arguing*.) But when Keats writes :

> Heard melodies are sweet, but those unheard
> Are sweeter. . . .

---

[1] Thus the "tinkled like iron" of his often quoted skating scene.

L

he is singing. And he sings so well that his muse rewards
him with a most marvellous find of rhythmical intuition.
For in this phrase, in the interlacing of *heard* and *un-
heard* with *sweet* and *sweeter* and the placing of these
words at the points of main stress, in the prolongation of
the line over the beginning of the following line, a prolongation " harmonised " by that of *sweet* into *sweeter*,
and in I know not what subtle rhythmical sympathy
which pervades it all, there is a most haunting suggestion
of the " leaf fringed " decoration which festoons round
the Grecian urn. The impression is heightened by the
proximity of the festooning sentence to the series of
questions which end the previous stanza. This series is
an admirable rhythmical rendering of the *motif* of gods
and maidens loth dancing round the vase. No more
faithful rendering of the dancing figures could be
dreamt than that succession of loose, yet connected in-
terrogating sentences, bounding one after the other in
" mad pursuit " :

> What men or gods are these ? What maidens loth ?
> What mad pursuit ? What struggle to escape ?
> What pipes and timbrels ? What wild extasy ?

There is the scene. It is not described. It is not interpreted. It is there, dancing before our eyes.

Scores of similar cases of rhythmical intuition might
be gleaned here and there in the rich fields of English
poetry. This phrase :

> . . . Pourest thy full heart
> In profuse strains of unpremeditated art

is not a description of the skylark singing, but the bird's

own song, rhythmically guessed by the poet.   When
Shakespeare sings :

> That time of year thou may'st in me behold
> When yellow leaves, or none, or few, do hang
> Upon those boughs which shake against the cold . . .

the broken rhythm of his second line—or none, or few . . .
—suggests the leaf here and the leaf there that remain
hanging in late autumn, witness of the foliage lost.   And
in that Ode to the West Wind, every line of which might
be quoted here for its rhythmical significance, how truly
felt and rendered the flight of leaf after leaf after leaf
in this succession of epithets :

> Yellow, and black, and pale, and hectic red,

suddenly gathered together by the wind in one heap as
the whole weight of the next sentence is gathered and
heaped in its first syllable :

> Pestilence-stricken multitudes ! . . .

We shall look in vain for such gleams of intuition in
Wordsworth, and the reason is that in Wordsworth
nature is not rendered but commented upon, talked
about, told, and at best represented.   He is generally
held to be the poet of nature *par excellence*, and if by
this is meant the poet who most frequently and willingly
and predominantly dwelt on nature, the claim holds
good.   But though he covered more ground and covered
it more conscientiously and minutely than any other
English poet, he is as a poet of nature inferior to Shakespeare and Milton, Blake and Shelley, unless we are to
judge by quantity and not by quality.   He is inferior as

a poet of nature because he is inferior as a poet. He can describe a landscape and the feelings which it arouses in his soul—or rather, *aroused*, for he generally speaks of the past—with most felicitous phrase. One thing he cannot do is to recreate it. And this, after all, the power of creation, is the only standard by which claims to poetic eminence can be judged. Considerable stress is laid on the accuracy of his knowledge of nature down to its minutest details. His poems, and Dorothy Wordsworth's diaries, amply show how acute were *their* powers of observation, for in this stage of his work, Dorothy must be considered a regular collaborator of her brother. It is doubtful, however, whether this kind of observation is a faculty that can be unreservedly praised in a poet. At any rate, it is not a merit in itself any more than a detailed knowledge of the human body down to the arcana of skin physiology is a merit in a sculptor. His eye is as scientifically accurate as the lens of an optical apparatus, a fact which certainly contributes to that photographic impression which his treatment of landscape conveys. He can give a most lovely literary description, or as it is said to-day, " pen-picture," of nature's face, but he is seldom if ever able to thrust a dart of intuition at nature's heart—such lightnings of poetry as :

> Tiger, tiger, burning bright
> In the forests of the night.

He had a penetrating, almost a mystic, feeling for nature, which gives quality to everything he wrote and makes it worth reading. But a feeling is not a poem. It is not even poetry. The following lines from the First

Book of the " Excursion" have been given as an example
of his natural mysticism :

> The clouds were touched,
> And in their silent faces did be read
> Unutterable love. Sound needed none,
> Nor any voice of joy ; his spirit drank
> The spectacle : sensation, soul, and form,
> All melted into him ; they swallowed up
> His animal being ; in them did he live,
> And by them did he live ; they were his life.
> In such access of mind, in such high hour
> Of visitation from the living God,
> Thought was not ; in enjoyment it expired.

An excellent statement, an excellent explanation of a
state of mysticism in the presence of a natural spectacle.
But the mysticism spoken of, referred to, restated, is not
there. In this passage, sober, painstaking, accurate,
there is no particular feeling of enjoyment, and thought,
far from " expiring," is omnipresent.

This contrast between the manner and the matter is
typical of Wordsworth. His method is indirect. Not
nature, but about nature, not poetic feeling, but about
poetic feeling. His literature is poetry " once removed,"
a reflection of poetry on the brain. Nowhere do we get
the first spontaneous promptings of his really poetic soul.
All he gives us is an account of them, sifted by his ever-
active intellect. Curiously enough this, the most autobiographical of writers, is the writer who gives least of
himself. The conscious Wordsworth is far too often in
his poetry. The subconscious Wordsworth is hardly ever
in it. Is there one single poem in which he sang un-
guardedly, unless it be the Lucy sequence, the most

mysterious and impressive of them all? It was not un-advisedly that he chose for his favourite methods the descriptive, the narrative and the autobiographical. They are the literary activities which best allow of an external, that is, an intellectual, treatment. No other treatment was normally possible to a writer who chose to remain at a sufficient distance from nature to be able to use it for his own ends and purposes.

But what are these ends and purposes? We have seen that the way to approach the study of Wordsworth's poetry is through an examination of the poet's mood while engaged in composition. We have observed that this mood is too intellectual and cold, and therefore results in irregularity and " patchiness " of form and poverty and inaccuracy of rhythm. But we still have to account for the strange fact that, though obviously born with the vision and sensibility of a great poet, Words-worth allowed his emotion to cool down and his intellect to " meddle " where it could not but freeze the warm embrace of the muses. The answer to this question is perhaps to be found in the arcana of temperament and race. But for our present purpose it is sufficient to show that Wordsworth rarely wrote in a wholly disinterested poetical mood. If all through his work we see the cold glare of his eye contemplating the agitation below as the eye of a general his regiments in battle, it is because, like a general, Wordsworth is intent on victory. His aim is beyond the poetical movements of his soul. He wants to study this ; he is after proving that ; he would illus-trate this feeling ; he would draw that lesson. For this reason, not merely his Lyrical Ballads but all save a handful of his poems, fail as poems. They are not constructions, but scaffoldings. Their meaning is beyond them, their soul is out of them. They are like ill-balanced pieces of sculpture ; they do not stand by themselves, and lean as it were on wooden props.

For a poem is a unit of beauty. It is a crystal of emotion, a creation having that beauty in unity and that unity in beauty which only inspiration can impart. Such unity is no mere condition or quality, the presence of which in a poem may be praised, the absence merely deplored. It is the very essence of the poem. It is the poem itself. No doubt it may vary in kind, according to author, mood or subject. Thus " Lycidas," though somewhat vacillating in composition, yet achieves a wonderful unity as a symphonic piece, thanks to the consistency in the development of the musical theme, which is defined in the opening sentence with as much clearness as is the theme of Beethoven's Fifth Symphony in its first two bars. Thus Spenser's " Prothalamion," though a mere " pièce de circonstance," is beautiful because *one* in its style and in the river-like harmony of its flow, so skilfully marked by the recurring refrain :

> Against the bridal day, which is not long ;
> Sweet Thames, run softly, till I end my song.

Thus Hamlet, not so much a tragedy as a dramatic poem, loose and uncentred as it seems, finds its unity in the subtle sympathy between the movement of the play and that of the Prince's soul where light and clouds come and go as in April skies. Thus the " Ode to the West Wind," as free as the impetuous element which it sings, is yet

one of the most architectural poems in the English language, a perfect union of inspiration and form.

But, except for a few of his less guarded utterances—
in which he shows how great a poet he might have been
—Wordsworth never succeeds in casting his thoughts
into one beautiful mould. The unity of each of his
works, as well as the unity of his work as a whole, is not
æsthetic, but philosophical and moral.

If, then, Wordsworth was rarely loved by the muses,
the reason is that he was not sufficiently devoted to them.
As a worshipper of Beauty he was neither whole-hearted
nor trustful enough. He sought to harness Pegasus to
the chariot of thought, not only because he was afraid
of the winged horse's " fancy," but because a cart is a
cart and one can always drive it on useful errands. At
bottom, he is too utilitarian, too much in a hurry. He
wants results, immediate results, from his cult to the
muses. And the muses, like all God-like beings, demand
disinterested hearts, and only to trustful and disinterested
hearts do they grant the gift of creation.

WORDSWORTH AND TRUTH

"His [Wordsworth's] hold over many thoughtful and, generally, mature minds is due to his having avowedly and, often also, practically, made truth his primary object, beauty being only second."

PROFESSOR LEGOUIS.
"Wordsworth."
The Cambridge History of
English Literature.

THAT beauty was not Wordsworth's primary concern we are all agreed. But it is not so sure that it was truth which occupied the first place in his heart.

There is undoubtedly a sense in which Wordsworth is, or seems to be, in the words of de Quincey " a truth-speaker of the severest literality." Whenever he deals with external, material facts, he is meticulously accurate. No poet seems to take more care not to mislead the reader about the " facts of the case." His footnotes are abundant, painstaking, full of solicitude. The sense of a line is explained, the origin of a legend is recorded, the date of an event is supplied, the allusion to a natural phenomenon is made clear. All the paraphernalia of " reality " wherewith his poems are built is disclosed. The poet seems to fear lest his readers think he is inventing or exaggerating. No! His feet are solid on the ground, and he shows the footprints on the road.

This accumulation of detail seems at first to be connected with that solicitude for accuracy of statement so prevalent in England; and no doubt, to a certain extent, it is so. We should not, however, forget that Wordsworth, for all his material accuracy, took considerable liberties with the *facts* when "staging" his poems. We are in a position to judge this feature of his work by comparing some of his poems with the raw material of which they are made, as preserved for us in the Journals of Dorothy Wordsworth. We would mention, for instance, "The Daffodils," "Resolution and Independence" and "Alice Fell." No one would dream of denying the poet the right to present his matter as best he chose. Yet it may be noticed that, since the alterations which Wordsworth made in his subject-matter were of the same order as, and even of a more important order than, the facts which he supplied in abundance, his profuseness of detail cannot be due to mere regard for accuracy of statement and fidelity to events.

It really is the direct outcome of his intellectual treatment. The intellect can only proceed by analysis. The synthetic manner is the privilege of poets, and only under inspiration can it be successfully attempted. Wordsworth cannot create. He delineates. He accumulates details in the hope that their sum arithmetic may produce the whole. He is the precursor of the present-day scientific and naturalistic literature, which claims to be accurate but is really dead.

⁂

But, it might be argued, his treatment of detail matters little. What matters is the substance of his poems. All we can ask of his sense of truth is that he should faithfully set in them the stone of experience picked up on his road.

It is doubtful, however, whether under this heading Wordsworth's sense of truth can be easily vindicated. Coleridge was the first to notice what he calls Words-

worth's " mental bombast," which he defines as " a disproportion of thought to the circumstance and occasion."
He gives three examples, namely, the lines :

> They flash upon that inward eye
> Which is the bliss of solitude

in "The Daffodils," the over-indignant apostrophe in
"Gypsies" and the well-known lines to the Child in
the ode :

> Thou best philosopher, who yet dost keep
> Thy heritage, thou eye among the blind,
> That, deaf and silent, read'st the eternal deep,
> Haunted for ever by the eternal mind,
>> Mighty prophet ! Seer blest !—
>> On whom those truths do rest
> Which we are toiling all our lives to find,
> In darkness lost, the darkness of the grave ;
> Thou, over whom thy Immortality
> Broods like the Day, a master o'er a slave,
> A presence which is not to be put by !

And though Coleridge declares that he knows no other
cases, many more could be found. We have referred to
the first line of the " Skylark." In a sense the whole ode on
Immortality is conceived in a mood of mental bombast.
The last stanza of " The Anecdote for Fathers " :

> O dearest, dearest boy ! my heart
> For better lore would seldom yearn,
> Could I but teach the hundredth part
> Of what from thee I learn,

is an obvious case of overstrained feeling which the trivial
anecdote hardly justifies.

Curiously enough Coleridge, who so aptly defines this
typical defect of Wordsworth's poetry, does not furnish

any explanation of it. Yet such an explanation suggests
itself at once. In these cases, Wordsworth is " working
himself up " into a passion or an emotion which he does
not actually feel. He is putting to a hard use that
" ability of conjuring up in himself passions which are
indeed far from being the same as those produced by
real events " of which he speaks in his definition of the
poet. But it is only nature that gives the true note.
Wordsworth is often overstrained because, though
sincere, he is not, in the poetic sense of the word, true.

It is at this point that the Annette episode must be
mentioned. Wordsworth, the most autobiographical of
poets, never refers to that subject in his works. The
facts of the case, recently unearthed, prove that he
behaved all through this adventure and its consequences,
exactly as might be expected from a man of so pure a
soul and so lofty a mind. But when we have absolved
him as a gentleman, we are at liberty to condemn him
as a poet. " The Prelude " was avowedly a poem destined
to trace the growth of his own mind through experience
and to narrate " his travels, hopes, aspirations, dis-
appointments and distresses, his inward conflicts and
perplexities." Is it conceivable, in the name of poetic
truth, that an episode so essential in the formation of
the poet's mind as his first conflict with sex should be
omitted from such a poem ? The point need hardly be
developed. In so far as this all-important episode is
absent from the Prelude, the Prelude is poetically false,
and its author, as a truth-seeker, stands condemned.

Though not always true to his experience, however,
Wordsworth may be true to his thought.

Of the three divinities of our everlasting Olympus, Beauty reveals herself spontaneously to pure worshippers ; Virtue, far from our hands, is yet always in sight, and the eyes of our soul are all we need to go towards her. Truth only stands occult behind infinite veils, and we must grope towards her secret abode, like blind men, up hill, through sheer effort. Truth requires vigour in her worshippers, and an unswerving concentration of endeavour. But she requires also, as does Beauty—perhaps in an even more exacting way—undivided allegiance, and above all, a fearless heart. For when all the veils are lifted, for all we know, Truth may be terrible.

It is doubtful whether Wordsworth was vigorous enough, courageous enough, single-hearted enough, to count as one of the great truth-seekers of the world. He is mentally much less vigorous and steady than is generally assumed. It is well known that he passed from one extreme to the other in his literary opinions on poetic diction, as a comparison between his earliest works and his Lyrical Ballads will show ; and that, moreover, he never applied his literary doctrines in an intelligible and consistent manner. It is also known that his critical faculty was mediocre,[1] and that he was anything but lucid in the exposition of his poetical principles—witness

---

[1] Cf. 'Reminiscences,' November, 1843.

"Wordsworth holds the critical power very low, infinitely lower than the inventive ; and he said to-day that if the quality of time consumed in writing critiques on the works of others were given to original composition, of whatever kind it might be, it would be much better employed ; it would make a man find out sooner his own level, and it would do infinitely less mischief. A false or malicious criticism may do much injury to the minds of others ; a stupid invention, either in prose or verse, is quite harmless."

The last sentence is highly instructive. It seems to give ground for the opinion that Wordsworth did not "hold the critical faculty infinitely lower than the inventive" from any sense of their intrinsic relative values, but perhaps, though unconsciously, from a feeling of his own inability as a critic.

his laborious definition of the Poet.[1] His political and philosophical opinions underwent similar changes, and, though studious and hard-working, he does not seem ever to have arrived at a consistent system of thought, nor, what is more to the point, to have sought one. His endeavour was to find peace and happiness, not *to understand*. His thoughts are often penetrating, but his thought is confused. Out of his poetry it is difficult to draw any clear conclusion ; the most it can yield is a vague impression of lofty, yet not very self-sure, optimism. Of his philosophy, as of his poetry, it may be said that it is a mist or an all-pervading atmosphere rather than a well-constructed scheme of definite units of beauty or truth, poems or ideas. On the question which is the bedrock of all philosophy, his solution is Holy Writ. Yet some of his less-guarded utterances express all the stoical gloom of a grim pantheism :

> No motion has she now, no force ;
>   She neither hears nor sees ;
> Roll'd round in earth's diurnal course,
>   With rocks, and stones, and trees.

His faith seems to be as cold and intellectual as his poetry, and unable really to illumine his inmost self. There is no truly religious poem in the whole mass of his work, though the whole of it is as it were interwoven with philosophical deism. A poet possessed of a faith so sure as he would have us (and himself) believe, would for ever live above the sombre melancholy of his effusion upon the Death of James Hogg :

> How fast has brother followed brother
> From sunshine to the sunless land. . . .

[1] Quoted in note, p. 136.

His assertions of faith, we feel, are self-protective. His business, as Matthew Arnold says, is *how to live*, and the *why live*, the *whence* and *whither* of life, must be kept off the mind as wolves off the cottage. Hence nature, the moral law, our common humanity, and even intimations from our early childhood, all available material in fact, is piled up in front of the door.

As he himself let out with disarming *naïveté* :

My whole life I have lived in pleasant thought.

We prefer to be guided by this unguarded confession rather than follow the ingenious but elaborate readings of his life which would represent him as tortured day and night by the problems of good and evil, of man and destiny. That Wordsworth was a sincere lover of man no one can doubt. That his heart suffered and bled for human evils, his works, his nature, and the evidence of his contemporaries preclude us from believing. Of this more hereafter. But this much may be said at once, that his " suffering " was a purely intellectual mood which he admirably described and illustrated, endowed as he was in such eminent degree with the gift of psychological interpretation.

Had he felt more deeply, he would have been unable to write with accents of such evident sincerity :

Far from the world I walk, and from all care.

This was his main purpose, and this he set out to achieve. There is no doubt that his efforts were crowned with success. Considering the troublous times in which he lived—troublous for body and soul—his achievement implies a considerable talent for self-defence, not devoid now and then of courage and determination. His mental life bears a striking resemblance to his material life. Just as he managed to protect his material peace against the troubles of the age by secluding himself in the most pleasing recesses of nature, so he succeeded in protecting his spiritual peace by living wrapped " in pleasant thought." Crags and precipices no doubt there were, in his mental as in his material retreat ; but they only added to the pleasures of the wanderer, who in his ramblings through thought or field knew how to border the abyss without danger. It would perhaps be unfair to say that Wordsworth withdrew from the world and from all care deliberately and consciously, much as a passage in the "Excursion" might tempt us to do so.[1] But then, our unconscious abstentions mould our life as much as our conscious activities, just as the hollows no less than the volumes of the body mould its form. There are here and there in Wordsworth lines which show how close was his watch over his peace and happiness :

> A day it was when I could bear
> Some fond regrets to entertain ;
> With so much happiness to spare
> I could not feel a pain.[2]

[1] Acknowledgments of gratitude sincere
Accompanied these musings ; fervent thanks
For my own peaceful lot and happy choice :
A choice that from the passions of the world
Withdrew, and fixed me in a still retreat,
Sheltered, but not to social duties lost ;
Secluded, but not buried ; and with song
Cheering my days, and with industrious thought,
With ever-welcome company of books,
By virtuous friendship's soul-sustaining aid,
And with the blessings of domestic love.

[2] Anecdote for Fathers.

Here is the secret of his forced optimism. Whenever he feels that truth is going to disturb his life of pleasant thought he unconsciously alters the course of his poem. He has that love of life, clean, simple, almost animal in its innocence, which distinguishes the British race. It is a healthy instinct which derives sufficient comfort for the riddles of life from the self-assertive strength of life itself, and which, when thoughts become importune, suppresses them with a flow of sensations by a mere act of the body.

> I well remember that those very plumes,
> Those weeds, and the high spear-grass on that wall,
> By mist and silent rain-drops silvered o'er,
> As once I passed, did to my heart convey
> So still an image of tranquillity,
> So calm and still, and looked so beautiful
> Amid the uneasy thoughts which filled my mind,
> That what we feel of sorrow and despair
> From ruin and from change, and all the grief
> The passing shows of being leave behind,
> Appeared an idle dream that could not live
> Where meditation was. I turned away,
> And walked along my road in happiness.[1]

Yet all is not physical in this protective instinct, so typically strong in the British race, so weak for example in the Russian. Just as all plants, though living, are not food for the body, so all truths, though living, are not food for the mind. Healthy races, like healthy individuals, have an instinct for the selection of nutritious, or rather for the rejection of poisonous truths, truths which overburden the soul with sorrow and take away

[1] "Excursion." Book I.

from it the taste for life. Such instinct Wordsworth possessed in an eminent degree, and therein, no less than in his respectability, he was representative of the British race, and particularly of the British gentleman. It is indeed a quality in a man; it is a defect in a truth-seeker.

❦

Most of Wordsworth's poems, particularly those in which the purpose is more manifest, suffer from this unconscious limitation of his outlook. A typical example is the poem generally known to-day as "The Leech-Gatherer," but perhaps more accurately described under its old title, "Resolution and Independence." Here is a comfortable country gentleman, " a traveller upon the moor," who, for sheer excess of joy, is suddenly seized by a fit of depression. He comes upon a poor old man.

> The oldest man he seemed that ever wore grey hairs,

so old and life-beaten that

> His body was bent double, feet and head
> Coming together in life's pilgrimage.

The gentleman inquires :

> What occupation do you there pursue?

He is a leech-gatherer. That is his occupation.

> Employment hazardous and wearisome.

A striking contrast. All fortune's smiles on one side. All fate's burdens on the other. Our poet might have been impressed with the view of life which the old man would have contemplated had he known all the facts; or he might have risen above the two sides and reflected

on the futility of it all, and exclaimed with La Bruyère :
" On a honte d'être heureux en face de certaines misères."
But no. Our poet has *his* own world to put in order, his
own house to build, his own axe to grind. He has not a
single thought for the old man as he really is, and therefore not one single feeling for him. He immediately
starts thinking about himself with such self-centred dis-
traction that, as he says :

> The old man still stood talking by my side ;
> But now his voice to me was like a stream
> Scarce heard ; nor word from word could I divide,

and, *giving* him nothing, not even the courtesy of listening, he *takes* from him comfort for his fit of depression—his depression which was a mere surfeit of joy :

> and when he ended,
> I could have laughed myself to scorn to find
> In that decrepit man so firm a mind.
> " God ! " said I, " be my help and stay secure.
> I'll think of the leech-gatherer on the lonely moor ! "

It is impossible to carry the self-protective instinct
further. Who could successfully attack such a citadel
of pleasant thought ? For there was only one possible
way of extracting an optimistic impression from the
incident, and that was to concentrate on the " resolution
and independence " of the old man, and to suppress all
the painful thoughts and feelings which would have
grieved a more fraternal and less guarded heart at the
sight of such pathetic adversity.

It should be noticed, moreover, that in this poem
Wordsworth deliberately distorts reality in order to
adjust it to his preconceived plan. We know through

Dorothy Wordsworth's Journal that the meeting with the old man took place on the road to Grasmere, not " on the lonely moor." As Professor Raleigh says, " Wordsworth shifts the scene in order to show the old man at his work, and to set him among elemental powers akin to his majestic and indomitable spirit." In doing so, the poet was within his rights. He was in fact showing great dramatic skill. But the eminent critic adds : " For the rest, the record is true enough," and here it is, I am afraid, impossible to agree with him. Far from being " true enough," the poem differs from the facts in one essential respect, namely, that the " resolution and independence " of which Wordsworth made the substance of his poem only existed in his imagination. The leech-gatherer of the poem says that leeches have become scarce,

> Yet still I persevere and find them where I may.

But let us turn to Dorothy Wordsworth who had no poem to write and no lesson to teach :

> " His trade was to gather leeches, but now leeches were scarce, and he had not strength for it. He lived by begging, and was making his way to Carlisle, where he should buy a few godly books to sell." [1]

Begging is not independence, and " not having strength for it " is not resolution. It will be seen therefore that Wordsworth " made up " not merely the scenery but the very substance of his poem. No one would find fault with this, were he engaged in a purely æsthetic task. But that is not the case. " Resolution and Independence " was written *in order to* justify optimism by means of

[1] Dorothy Wordsworth's Journal. October 3rd, 1800.

feelings supposed to be taken from nature. Fidelity to nature is, and must be, on his own theory, the first condition of Wordsworth's work. In this case the image supplied by nature was so *refracted* by Wordsworth's brain as to appear upside down. The result is a false poem, a poem which, though professing to be born out of an emotion actually felt, is wholly invented—a typical example of that *cerebral* poetry in which Wordsworth habitually indulged, written in such a mood that the heart does not inspire the brain, but the brain forces and drives the heart to feeling. And that is why the "Leech-Gatherer," despite some passages of lofty eloquence, cannot be counted as a work of art. It is an anecdote, deliberate, prejudiced and overstrained.

There are, however, cases where Wordsworth is still further from truth. "The Idiot Boy," for instance, is a poem of which it is difficult to speak in terms of moderation. In this work the poet aimed at "tracing the maternal passion through many of its more subtle windings." The mere choice of such a subject for the illustration of such a theory reveals an utter lack of delicacy which the treatment fully confirms. Wordsworth devoted a considerable part of his letter to John Wilson to the task of defending himself against those readers who objected to "The Idiot Boy" on the ground that "nothing is a fit subject for poetry which does not please." His defence may have been convincing to Mr. John Wilson, but it seems wholly irrelevant, since it is based on the assumption that the objections to this poem are only

grounded on (*a*) the word " idiot " and its associations ;
(*b*) the " loathing and disgust " which many people feel
at the sight of an idiot. But the real human objection
to such a subject and to its use for such a " demonstra-
tion " is far deeper than Wordsworth seems to have
realised. The existence of half-witted people is one of
the most painful facts for a mind sensitive and fraternal,
one of those subjects in which our common humanity
feels so hurt, so insulted and trampled upon, that it
awakes in us, indeed,

> The pangs that tempt the spirit to rebel.

Wordsworth comfortably speaks of " that sublime expression of scripture that *their* [the idiots'] *life is hidden
with God*," and hugs the fact that " Among the Alps,
where they are numerous, they are considered, I believe,
as a blessing to the family to which they belong."[1] This
is self-protection with a vengeance. It is the measure of
Wordsworth's capacity for imposing his optimism on the
most recalcitrant aspects of nature that he can turn this
subject into a debonair story and comment on it as
follows : " I wrote the poem with exceeding delight and
pleasure, and whenever I read it I read it with pleasure."[1]
His " tracing the maternal passion through many of its
more subtle windings " is so successful as to depict a
mother referring to her own half-witted child as " My
idiot boy " :

> Oh dear, dear pony, my sweet joy !
> Oh carry back my idiot boy !

This is pathetic, but not as Wordsworth meant it. And

[1] Letter to Mr. Wilson.

the end, that atrocious end, with its misplaced jocosity and its shameless exhibition of one of man's deepest and most inexplicable miseries, is the most painful blot that ever disfigured the work of a poet.

False to nature, " The Idiot Boy " is false to poetry. It is written by a mind which goes to nature disposed to find what it carries within its own self. It is predetermined, a foregone promise of fact for a foregone conclusion.

A similar observation applies in a greater or lesser degree to practically all Wordsworth's poetry. As a work of thought, no less than as a work of art, it is marred by the fact that the *purpose* of Wordsworth " is too much with us." His mental " milieu " is not passive to the light of nature, but on the contrary *refracts* it and therefore gives to things and people seen through his brain a shape all *his* own. An overpowering nature, he forces upon the objects which he absorbs the texture of his own mind. Hence, his powers of observation far exceed his achievements as a truth-seeker just as his powers of intuition exceed his achievements as a poet. In his philosophic, as in his poetic, capacity the effect can be perceived of that ever-vigilant consciousness directed to other ends, diverging, distracting, which all through his work bars spontaneity, nips the budding flower of inspiration and deviates thought on its way to truth.

As studies of truth his poems are no more satisfactory than as impressions of beauty. And for the same reason, that their centre of gravity is beyond them, outside of

beauty and outside of truth. For Wordsworth as a truth-
seeker is hindered, not merely by the disproportion
between his intellectual vigour and the magnitude and
scope of his subject, not merely by his self-protective
instinct against certain distasteful truths, but also by his
moral[1] preoccupation. The truth-worshipper in him is
no more single-hearted than the worshipper of beauty.
Truth like beauty is in his hands a mere instrument for
the achievement of a moral purpose. Hence, being both
of an absolute essence, they evade his grasp.

[1] We take this word in a wide sense, not merely as "moralising" nor
even as "ethical," but as "purposeful" and "useful" in the loftiest meaning of these adjectives.

WORDSWORTH AND VIRTUE

" I wish either to be considered as a teacher, or as nothing."

WILLIAM WORDSWORTH.

WORDSWORTH'S primary deity was neither Truth nor Beauty. It was Virtue. Now, if the Prince of Beauty is the Poet, and the Prince of Truth is the Philosopher, the Prince of Virtue is the Saint. No one, not even Wordsworthians, claim this high title for William Wordsworth. But there is a word, a beautiful word, which belongs to the kingdom of Virtue and which fits him admirably. Wordsworth was a Master.

A Master is something more and something less than a Sage. A Sage gives forth wisdom as the tree does apples, with calm passivity, knowing that whether they be plucked and eaten or fall to earth and rot, nothing is lost. A Master is less impassive and more impatient. Wisdom does not well up in him like sap from the roots of the tree, but is distilled in his mind by toil of heart and brain. Thus, wisdom is less personal than natural in the Sage; less natural than personal in the Master. Hence the Master's generous desire to share it with his fellow beings, for we are only eager to give what we feel to be truly our own.

Wordsworth was filled with this generous desire to benefit men with the wisdom distilled by his mind. He had a true vocation for teaching. When he says: " I wish either to be considered as a teacher, or as nothing," he is neither trying to smuggle his poetic wares under cover of utility, nor indulging in vain metaphor, but tersely expressing a literal truth. A volume might be collected of similar declarations in verse and prose all through his writings. But, had he not written one line on his intentions, his work would be a sufficient witness, an imposing witness of the earnestness with which he understood his didactic task.

He was eminently fitted for it both by his qualities and by his defects. He possessed that synthetic view of life which allowed him to see all in one and one in all, that spiritual essence which is to the trinity True-Good-Beautiful what the Godhead is to the Holy Trinity. It is this spiritual essence which pervades all his work and gives it a pre-poetical value, previous to and independent of all form and inspiration. In the loftiness and vastness of his synthetic intuition of things he is second to none among English poets, and ranks with Shakespeare and Shelley, above Milton, a giant prisoner in the beliefs of his age. It is his greatness as a seer which gives nobility and " harmony in numbers " to his longer and more ambitious works, and which, in " The Prelude " and " The Excursion," stands him in good stead when inspiration fails. He is a figure great enough to wear the drapery of eloquence.

❧

Thus gifted with the vision and the faculty divine, Wordsworth saw nature with *active* eyes. It is, I believe, to this spiritual gift, and not to his theories on diction and style, that he owes the distinction of having cleared English poetry from the excesses of " poetic diction." There is after all not much difference between *diction* and substance in poetry, and the word itself with its literal meaning of " saying " stands at the confluence of the matter and the manner of what is *said*. If Wordsworth succeeded in rendering English poetic style simpler than it had been it is mostly due to the fact that he had something to say. Yet it is perhaps possible to exaggerate his influence in this respect. Shelley and Keats were his juniors and read him, but it is not evident that they owe to him their own clearness and directness of diction. The sun of the French Revolution rose for all. The ebb of the rationalistic age set in for all. And both Shelley and Keats were superior to Wordsworth in literary craftsmanship.[1] The fact remains, however, that, chronologically at least, priority must go to Wordsworth. He represents in the history of English culture the discovery of nature, an event similar to the discovery of America in the history of action, resulting in the enlargement of the domain of the spirit to include a new continent of life.

In this historical function, Wordsworth, the master, is in my view much greater than Wordsworth the poet. As a poet his treatment of nature is too photographic, too realistic, too detailed. His knowledge of the facts of nature is too scientific and his presentation of them too matter-of-fact, too disconnected. Hence his influence upon English poetry may not have been all for the good. His accuracy in detailed statement and description acted as a powerful stimulant on the innate tendency of the race towards concreteness, which is in itself unpoetical, for it leaves no freedom of movement to the imagination, it disperses the attention over the surface of details and prevents the emotion from crystal-

[1] This was as much as recognised by Wordsworth himself when he said : "Shelley is one of the best *artists* of us all. I mean in workmanship of style." Opinions expressed in conversation with his nephew and biographer. 1827.

lising into form. His successors felt that they had to compete with a powerful specialist. Poets became too self-conscious to speak of "a bird upon a tree" and had to say "a thrush in the sycamore" even when, as is often the case, the vaguer expression was the more accurate rendering of the impression actually received. On the whole, Wordsworth seems to have deprived English poets of their old innocent and unsophisticated attitude towards nature, innocent even when extravagantly complicated. And, paradoxical as it may seem, by emphasising detail Wordsworth has indirectly fostered a new era of "poetic diction"; for the over-ornamented style of the English poetry of yesterday was in a measure the outcome of an effort to find on the surface of nature the poetical wealth which can only be gained by exploring its depths.

Victor Hugo is credited with being the first French poet who noticed that the light of the moon is blue. Wordsworth gives Cowper a bad mark for having said

> And *even* the boding owl
> That hails the rising moon has charms for me.

After Wordsworth, no such heresy is possible. His work is so self-observed, so accurate, so conscientious, that after him poetry becomes encumbered with subtle unwritten laws, analogous to the laws of good breeding and society, which are supposed to be known as a matter of course. Poetry becomes self-conscious and nature becomes incorporated into culture, hence into society. Every well-educated person feels bound to experience strong and original sensations in the presence of nature, and the audience to whom poets address themselves is fastidious and sophisticated.

As a master, however, Wordsworth is one of the most imposing writers of nature known to the world of letters. A constant, faithful, persevering worshipper, he made of earth, sea and sky, a glorious shrine, and of every plant animal and stone, a hallowed creature. This faith he expanded and taught in a work which for earnestness, elevation and that greatness which results from mere mass, has few parallels. Though he failed to sing nature, he explained it in words as felicitous, as noble and eloquent as were possible only to such a man in such surroundings. Had he been more of a poet he would have had a lesser influence—at least a less direct influence—as a preacher of nature on a people whose turn of mind is more concrete than symbolical, and whose imagination builds on sensations and actions rather than on feelings and thoughts. As it was, he wrote his Poem of Nature keeping as close to the original as he possibly could, and dwelling in a simple, eloquent, dignified yet not declamatory style on all the joys which body, heart and mind can reap from an intimate knowledge of meadows, hills, forests and skies. This treatment, vaguely poetical throughout, yet never or hardly ever really poetical, explains why Wordsworth should have been so successful in his great task, the wholesale conversion of his country to the religion of nature.

But in dwelling too often on Wordsworth as " the poet of nature " there is a risk of underestimating the fact that he was predominantly a student of man. There is indeed much to be said for the view that, had he not lived under the almost continuous influence of his sister, his philosophical and psychological tendency might have absorbed most of his power, leaving but little to devote to nature, its scenes and moods. At any rate it must be noticed that the centre of gravity of his thoughts is not in nature but in man, and that at bottom it is his interest in man that is the basis of his interest in nature. To my mind Wordsworth is at his best when exploring the recesses of his own soul, the part of creation with which he was most familiar. He has an exceptional gift for rendering that sensation of inner spaciousness which the word *soul* evokes :

> . . . when thy mind
> Shall be a mansion for all lovely forms,
> Thy memory be as a dwelling-place
> For all sweet sounds and harmonies. . . .[1]

But it is not necessary to go to his verse for instances of that feeling of mental space :

" There is also a meditative, as well as a human, pathos ; an enthusiastic, as well as an ordinary, sorrow ; a sadness that has its seat in the depths of reason, to which the mind cannot sink gently of itself—but to which it must descend by treading the steps of thought.[2]

This is marvellously said because marvellously felt and true. It is an example which illustrates the two Wordsworthian qualities, at first sight so contradictory, namely, the loftiness and comprehensiveness of his outlook and his acuteness in the perception of detail. There is little that he did not observe in the workings of the human

[1] Lines near Tintern Abbey.
[2] Essay supplementary to the Preface to the Poems (1815).

creature, little that he did not note down in his accurate and telling manner. And from his mode of life he derived an original mode of treating mental subjects, a kind of pictorial arranging of them which might be described as mental landscape painting. We must observe, however, that in his mental landscape painting, Wordsworth evinces the same external, photographic manner which we have noticed in his treatment of nature. It is in a way the style known in the language of the studio as Academic, or, as the French graphically put it, *pompier*. Wordsworth's shortcomings as psychologist are best explained by a comparison with Shakespeare. That the comparison is not crushing is a true measure of Wordsworth's greatness. The difference between them may be summed up in one word—creation. Shakespeare creates, and Wordsworth describes. Shakespeare lives in turn in each of his characters. Wordsworth forces his characters to take the form and movements which suit his particular theme or thesis. In the work of Shakespeare, his own psychology is absent, at least it can only be guessed by inference. In that of Wordsworth there is hardly any psychology but that of Wordsworth. Shakespeare gives life to his characters, sons and daughters of his spirit, and emancipates them, so that they live a life of their own in the world of posterity. Wordsworth wanders through nature and the mind with his tablets ready, and in his wanderings gathers and labels a most imposing collection of flowers, stones and insects of psychology. His characters do not live. They stay where they are placed. They are illustrations in a book. There is of course between Shakespeare and Wordsworth a difference in power. Shakespeare could create and

Wordsworth could not. But there is also a difference in attitude. Wordsworth would teach and Shakespeare would not.

Wordsworth and Shakespeare are thus the two poles of English poetry, the ethical and the æsthetical. All the other great names in English poetry partake in varying proportions of the nature of both Shakespeare and Wordsworth. This is conspicuously the case with Milton, and still more with Shelley. Shelley contains the greatest possible measure of Shakespeare and the greatest possible measure of Wordsworth that can be found in any English poet. True this double strain does not strike the eye in any outward likeness. Keats, not Shelley, is generally considered as the heir of Shakespeare. But though Keats has the voice, he has not the spirit of Shakespeare. Shelley, since Shakespeare, is the first to love nature not merely with his depth of *passion*, but also with that intensity of *action* only to be found where masculine vigour is wed to feminine sensibility. It is in this inner sense, not in any external likeness of line or manner, that Shelley is Shakespearean. And it is equally in an inner and spiritual sense that he is Wordsworthian, not in his doctrines, but in his strong didactic, purposeful bent of mind. Fortunately for poetry, Shelley's subconscious strength favoured the Shakespearean rather than the Wordsworthian strain in his nature ; but the traces of the struggle remain in all his poems and add to their inherent beauty that sense of unsatisfied yearning which only complex natures have fathomed in all its melancholy depth.

Wordsworth himself, in asking us to consider him as

teacher or as nothing, led us to expect that the defects of his psychology would be those attached—theoretically at least—to the teaching profession. And to begin with, he sees the world of men from a platform. Despite many professions of humility, the frequency of which is in itself significant, Wordsworth was deeply imbued with the sense of his own superiority. It pervades all his work, verse and prose ; it appears in his private life, in his manners, in his language, and even in his features. It forms the very basis of his criticism. It explains his quiet, passive resistance to unpopularity and his never abated self-confidence. It is indeed the very substance of his claim to be considered as a teacher or as nothing. When he now and then puts himself in the position of the humble student in the fifth form of Nature, as in the " Anecdote for Fathers," in " The Leech-Gatherer " or in " The Ode," he is merely indulging in what he would describe as " an artifice of composition." In his own eyes he is the great Poet who " ought to travel before men occasionally as well as at their sides."[1] He is, in fine, the teacher and therefore he looks down on other men as the school-master does on his schoolboys—with the purest and most devoted feelings, with a genuine and ardent desire to improve their minds and souls, but obviously from above.

This attitude of mind leads him into treating his characters as subjects for experiment. A typical example is the " Anecdote for Fathers," but, though clearer in this instance, the tendency is everywhere in his work. He does not grant his characters that respect which the grown-up gives the grown-up. He does not treat them on an equal footing. He looks through them, beyond

[1] Letter to Mr. Wilson,

them, or over their heads. He does not tell them where he is going. In his hands every human being becomes an object, an utensil. In the end a feeling grows that the writer's sympathy for man is more abstract and intellectual than actual and felt, and that his wonderful sensitiveness to mental movements is connected rather with acuity of perception than with genuine emotion and penetrating sympathy. He seems to arrive at fraternity as a logical conclusion of his meditations on man and nature, but fraternity does not well up from his heart.

He is singularly lacking in sense of humour, and as sense of humour is the only check to the pedantic tendency innate in didactic minds, it follows that Wordsworth often lays himself open to the charge of pedantry. It is, I believe, to his pedantry, his conscientious pedantry, and not to any professional meanness, that his ungenerous criticism of " The Ancient Mariner " must be attributed. For no man ever was less capable of deliberately causing pain to his enemies, let alone his most intimate friend.

All men do not seem able *to be themselves* in the same degree. Wordsworth was himself very much indeed. He was almost quite himself. It is not therefore surprising that he should have given so much of his vitality to his defects and weaknesses since he had enough to spare from that which he bestowed on his wonderful gifts and qualities. Hence, a rich personality, a splendid overgrowth of spirit.

It often happens that seeing in a forest a tree of exceptional dimensions and form we fancy it to be formed of two trees grown together. Thus Wordsworth has been sometimes explained as a double writer. Wordsworth the good and Wordsworth the bad—and the usual advice

to neophytes is to wade through his worthless shallow
waters and enjoy a bracing spiritual swim in his gorgeous
depths. Wordsworthians, however, as Matthew Arnold
reminds us, read everything the master wrote ; and if
to think that Wordsworth is one and indivisible is to be
a Wordsworthian, I humbly beg to be received into the
brotherhood. Inequality is possible in spontaneous
artists, careless in execution because quick to be impressed
and eager to put their emotion into form and pass on.
Such a type is Lope de Vega, with whom, on the ground
of their inequality, Professor Fitzmaurice Kelly compares
Wordsworth. But Wordsworth, as we know, is not a
spontaneous, still less a careless writer. He is a conscientious builder, working according to a consistent
plan and knowing exactly what he is aiming at.
There is no inequality in his work as he understood it.

His case becomes clear once the right interpretation
is given to his literary genius. He is usually considered
a poet, and as such, of course, he is unequal ; he lacks
unity, beauty, strength. But let him be restored to his
proper place. Let him be seen as a Master with a rich
substratum of poetical intuition and his work will recover
all the unity, excellence and strength with which it was
conceived. Then, and then only, shall we see, rising before
our eyes in all its majesty, the " body of the Gothic
church " with all the " minor pieces," " little cells,
oratories and sepulchral recesses ordinarily included in
those edifices." These minor pieces, which failed as
" poems " and as " experiments,"[1] find their balance as

[1] " The majority of the following poems are to be considered as experiments " (advertisement to the " Lyrical Ballads." 1798). Here the word
is used in a restricted sense, i.e. experiments in simple diction, but it may
be extended to its usual scientific meaning in view of what Wordsworth
often wrote on the matter.

" short essays,"[1] lessons, steps and exercises towards the improvement of men and the refining and elevating of their souls. Inspiration shines—an " accident "—here and there. Truth shows here and there her austere face. But the sole unity of the vast work is in its stern, lofty, never flinching *purpose*. It is this word which comes most naturally under Wordsworth's pen. It is the impulse that was ever awake in his soul. It is the strength that kept going the steady step of the Wanderer.

He wrote in verse. Yes. But he was explicit enough as to the place he granted to " metre " in his " composition." It was an adventitious and superadded element. It was an afterthought. A happy afterthought, it must be recognised, for, though mere verse owes little to him, he owes much to mere verse. Wordsworth was singularly poor in the gift of form. He is great and formless like the sea. Had he not written in verse, his work would probably have spread as do waters at the mercy of gravity. As it is Wordsworth found ready-made forms in the English language which saved his message from perishing, drowned in a verbal flood. That is why he is at his best when most closely held by the mould of verse which he has chosen. Even his blank verse, though leaving him at liberty to flow, at least banks him like a river. In his ballads the difficulties of English versification, and especially of rhyming, are a brake, not always effective enough, on his profuseness. But where he is best is

Within the sonnet's scanty plot of ground.

He did no more than pay a debt of gratitude when he wrote the praise of the sonnet, for, in a literary sense,

---

[1] Wordsworth uses the word in his "Observations."

there is no doubt that he described his own soul when he
spoke of

> . . . some souls (for such there needs must be)
> Who have felt the weight of too much liberty.

From this point of view, verse must be considered as
an important element of Wordsworth's work. But that
he wrote in verse is not in itself sufficient to establish
that he wrote in a poetical mood. As long as he taught
he was indifferent to what he felt. We can watch him
pass with his usual calm step from the inspired to the
uninspired mood by comparing the two sonnets which
he wrote on the spinning-wheel. The first of them is a
real poem, full of the music of the wheel :

> Grief, thou hast lost an ever-ready friend
> Now that the cottage spinning-wheel is mute ;
> And care—a comforter that best could suit
> Her froward mood, and softliest reprehend ;
>
> And love—a charmer's voice, that used to lend,
> More efficaciously than aught that flows
> From harp or lute, kind influence to compose
> The throbbing pulse,—else troubled without end ;
>
> Even joy could tell, joy craving truce and rest
> From her own overflow, what power sedate
> On those revolving motions did await
>
> Assiduously, to soothe her aching breast—
> And—to a point of just relief—abate
> The mantling triumphs of a day too blest.

These pauses after *grief* and *care* and *love*, followed by
long sentences, are exquisite renderings of the momentum
of the revolving wheel ; " assiduously " is a triumph of
insight into the psychological effect of the reiterating
movements of the wheel with its constant returning ;

and the delicate thoughts expressed, rather than recorded, seem to be spun out as the sonnet turns on quietly
on its own axle. But for Wordsworth, the following
prosaic and prosy sermon had exactly the same value :

> Excuse is needless when with love sincere
> Of occupation, not by fashion led,
> Thou turn'st the wheel that slept with dust o'erspread ;
> *My* nerves from no such murmur shrink—though near,
>
> Soft as the dorhawk's to a distant ear,
> When twilight shades bedim the mountain's head.
> She who was feigned to spin our vital thread
> Might smile, O lady ! on a task once dear
>
> To household virtues. Venerable art,
> Torn from the poor ! Yet will kind Heaven protect
> Its own, not left without a guiding chart,
>
> If rulers, trusting with undue respect
> To proud discoveries of the intellect,
> Sanction the pillage of man's ancient heart.

Because, when contemplating the initial fact of experience which soaked into his poetical intuition and
moved him to work, the overpowering impulse which
determined the shape and direction of the poem was his
purpose. Strong and self-controlled as he was, he could
not alter the architecture of his spirit, and in his spirit
the triangle True-Good-Beautiful was placed with its
Good point up. The Good was his strongest tendency,
and he had to obey it. He was above all an ethical nature,
and every other tendency in him was curbed to the service
of his ethical impulse. His work cannot be understood
unless it is considered mainly as an *act*. Poor in beauty,
hesitating in truth, it is a masterpiece of purpose and
intention.

CONCLUSION

I MAY perhaps be permitted to say that in this, his pre-dominant devotion to Virtue, Wordsworth is the proto-type of the British race and civilisation. In him, as in the average Briton, the moral comes first, and the poetical and the scientific take what remains. And starting from this main feature, a portrait could be drawn which, by delineating Wordsworth's character, would almost exactly fit any other gentleman of his nation. For this tendency towards Virtue—that is towards good in action, under-stood as covering all the range of the human spirit, from its highest to its lowest, from the heroic to the narrowly utilitarian—is the key to the understanding of British character.

In Wordsworth we can see it at work. It reaches but once the heroic pitch, when in the ardour of youth he thinks of saving France from anarchy by offering himself as a leader to the French—and the lack of judgment that his idea revealed takes nothing from its heroism. It is still on a noble and elevated plane when it inspires his courageous Tract against the Convention of Cintra. But it finds its middle and steadiest position in the exer-cise of moral action as applied to the social conditions reigning at the time and which are as it were the raw matter of conduct. Wordsworth takes good care to record the point when referring to his seclusion :

> In a still retreat
> Sheltered, but not to social duties lost.

This social-moral, we might say political, attitude is ever present in his work, from its highest flights of political eloquence to its humblest tasks of parish-pump life, such as are fulfilled nowadays by the public-spirited citizens who write letters to the papers. The following sonnet, for instance, is nothing else than a letter to " The Times " in " metre " :

On the Projected Kendal and Windermere Railway

Is there no nook of English ground secure
From rash assault ?   Schemes of retirement sown
In youth, and 'mid the busy world kept pure
As when their earliest flowers of hope were blown,
Must perish ; how can they this blight endure ?
And must he too the ruthless change bemoan
Who scorns a false utilitarian lure
'Mid his paternal fields at random thrown ?
Baffle the threat, bright scene, from Orrest head
Given to the pausing traveller's rapturous glance :
Plead for thy peace, thou beautiful romance
Of nature ; and, if human hearts be dead,
Speak, passing winds ; ye torrents, with your strong
And constant voice, protest against the wrong.

Wordsworth is therefore one of the creators of modern public opinion, that real government of Great Britain. But public opinion does not limit its sway to strictly political issues. It forms a powerful body of unwritten laws which govern life much more directly and continually than Acts of Parliament. Wordsworth is one of the " unacknowledged legislators " of this book of unwritten laws which extend to all matters of opinion, taste and culture, and in him we can find the main features of the nineteenth-century Englishman. We have just seen his letter to " The Times." Here is his page of Baedeker.

THE LAST SUPPER, BY LEONARDO DA VINCI,
IN THE REFECTORY OF THE CONVENT OF
MARIA DELLA GRAZIA, MILAN

Though searching damps and many an envious flaw
Have marred this work, the calm ethereal grace,
The love deep-seated in the Saviour's face,
The mercy, goodness, have not failed to awe
The elements : as they do melt and thaw
The heart of the beholder—and erase
(At least for one rapt moment) every trace
Of disobedience to the primal law.
The annunciation of the dreadful truth
Made to the twelve, survives : lip, forehead, cheek,
And hand reposing on the board in ruth
Of what it utters, while the unguilty seek
Unquestionable meanings, still bespeak
A labour worthy of eternal youth !

It is from this social-moral tendency, so deep in him, that Wordsworth's literary utilitarianism derives, that is, his desire to apply his ideas and emotions to some useful purpose. To work, think or feel " in the air " is contrary to Wordsworth's nature as it is to that of every Englishman. He feels, as do his countrymen, the necessity of incarnating his thought, and thus his social-moral tendency merges into the bodily or material tendency, also typical of his race. Wordsworth is an excellent example of that materialism—not of thought, but of instinct—which leads the Briton towards preferring to all other activities manifestation in the tangible world. Physically, it shows itself in his splendid animal vitality which inspires so many telling lines in his poetry—particularly in "The Prelude"—as to make quotation unnecessary, and in the cleanliness and innocence of his sense of pleasure —for the body is innocent and cannot sin. Mentally, it appears in what Coleridge called his "matter-of-factness," a certain inability to rise into the realm of the spirit and to part company with "flesh and blood";[1] a certain pedestrian turn of mind which is somewhat connected with that other British characteristic, empiricism. It is also from the social-moral stem that his very British power of self-control derives, since self-control presupposes action, *an aim*, a purpose. And this, the British virtue *par excellence*, is the bane of Wordsworth's poetry, for, though neither all nor perhaps the best poetry is written when overflowing with Dionysian spirits, it is doubtful whether a mind that never was possessed by Dionysos can rise to poetry at all. The British gentleman and the poet are ever in conflict within Wordsworth's soul. Generally, the British gentleman wins.

We reach then a plausible explanation for the three facts noticed by Matthew Arnold. That Wordsworthians are right in reading everything Wordsworth wrote is, we have seen, another way of saying that there is only *one* Wordsworth. All that he wrote, even "Vaudracour and Julia," which Matthew Arnold did not read, is worth reading, since all, when rightly understood, finds its

[1] "I have wished to keep the reader in the company of flesh and blood, persuaded that by so doing I shall interest him." Preface to "Lyrical Ballads."

place in a work of great and impressive literary unity. This fact becomes evident as soon as the centre of gravity of Wordsworth's work is seen to be where it ought always to have been, not in Poetry, but in Teaching. Then the whole perspective becomes clear and the fact that some of his essays in metre are more distinctly poetical than others is restored to the insignificance which it had in the eyes of their author and of his followers.

The same fact explains why Wordsworth is not a universal poet, since essentially he is not a poet. His eyes are fixed on Virtue, and of Beauty he sees nothing but the light that falls on Virtue's face. His literature, admirable though it is, does not reach that pitch of intensity which moves the stranger. It is a literature essentially national in its tone, temper and general trend, a " criticism of life," sober, positive and well-meaning. It lacks the fire of passion and the glow of beauty and the splendour of form. It occupies a zone equidistant from poetry and philosophy. Though in verse, it is essentially prosaic not only in its *key* and in its self-consciousness but in the intellectual mood of the treatment, which allows and even requires the use of methods of style peculiar to the essayist—the underlining of certain words, quotations, literary allusions—forbidden to the poet not by any academic laws but by the very nature of inspiration. It is a *genre* which admirably fits the national taste for a literature in which no particular essence predominates, which is thoughtful though not philosophical, well written though not poetical, edifying[1] though not avowedly moral, mixed and vague like life,

---

[1] Matthew Arnold " can read with pleasure and edification " all Wordsworth.

healthy, serious and above all useful. The difference between the national and the foreign estimate of Wordsworth is due precisely to the fact that everything he says is said in exactly that key which fits the British mental ear and thus is heard with the greatest possible mental resonance, while the same fact which multiplies his voice in his own country deadens it abroad. The national character of his genius explains the existence of Wordsworthians. Other great poets can go abroad unguarded. They risk nothing, or, if they do, it is a universal, not a national value. Wordsworth, however, represents a national asset, and Wordsworthians are his bodyguard. Hence their sensitiveness, since their worship is blended with that most sensitive of passions, national feeling.

Space and time are so closely knit together that it would be surprising if Wordsworth were to spread into posterity more surely than he does in universality. He has been considered in these pages as a representative of the British Gentleman, and it is not unadvisedly that the term *British*, and not *English*, has been applied to him. For in the British Gentleman the permanent features of his race are of course modified by transient shades, manners of being which belong to his age and will disappear with it. Wordsworth is much more deeply connected with the British Gentleman than was any other great English poet with the transient type of his race that happened to be his coeval. Chaucer does not resemble the Anglo-Norman Knight, Shakespeare the Elizabethan courtier, Milton the Puritan, as closely as Wordsworth the British Gentleman whom he incarnates, and even precedes and contributes to evolve. The British Gentleman is the result of an historical development which absorbs all these previous types and many more types of Anglo-Saxon manhood—from the City Merchant, already powerful in Chaucer's times, to the rough country squire whom Fielding represented with a gusto not altogether devoid of an almost fraternal sympathy. The romance of the Chaucerian Knight, the elegance of the Elizabethan courtier, the enterprise of the City Merchant, the robust vitality of the country squire, softened and polished by the growing influence of the English lady, fond of books and flowers and tea, all these elements survive in the complex personality of the British Gentleman and live together within him, not always in harmony, but nearly always in correct companionship.

Like all living beings, the British Gentleman must die. He will die to survive in a still more complex type which is being evolved under our eyes. Who does not see the far-reaching changes brought about in British manhood by the economic evolution of the twentieth century, by the closer relationship between Great Britain and the Anglo-Saxon nations overseas, by the growing intimacy with France which set in after the Fashoda incident had closed the period of political misunderstandings, and last but not least by the European War? When the new type of Englishman asserts itself and its tastes, it is safe to predict that of all the great names of English literature those will suffer most which will have most intimately and adequately represented the type that passed, and of them, Wordsworth is perhaps the first. His glory belongs to Great Britain and to the nineteenth century.

It is not the smaller for that. Duration and expansion are after all but gross conceptions, linked with man's two mental infirmities, space and time. Depth and power are great if only for one second, if only in one spot of space. Wordsworth's greatness is precisely in that which limits his appeal : in the fact that he represents his country and his age in a manner worthy of his country and of his age. That he is neither universal nor permanent detracts nothing from his symbolical value. Indeed, it adds perhaps to it. Are not Wordsworthians secretly pleased and flattered in their insularity when they think of Wordsworth as surrounded by seas of incomprehension ?

INDEX